wishing you a happy
40th - love from
John & Pauline
x

Improve Your Golf IQ

Improve Your Golf IQ

David Ayres and John Cook

Illustrations by Graham Gaches

David & Charles

First published in 2002 in the UK by
David & Charles
Brunel House
Newton Abbot
Devon

ISBN 0 7153 1395 9

QUAR.IGIQ

Conceived, designed and produced by
Quarto Publishing plc
The Old Brewery
6 Blundell Street
London N7 9BH

Senior project editor Nicolette Linton
Art editor Jill Mumford
Assistant art director Penny Cobb
Text editors Peter Kirkham, Alice Tyler
Designer Peter Laws
Illustrator Graham Gaches
Photographer Bob Atkins
Indexer Pamela Ellis

Art director Moira Clinch
Publisher Piers Spence

Manufactured by Universal Graphics, Singapore
Printed by Standard Industries (Pte) Ltd,
Singapore

9 8 7 6 5 4 3 2 1

Contents

Introduction

Golf should carry a public health warning. Once you experience the joy of striking a small, dimpled white ball into the blue yonder, your chances of not becoming addicted to the game are, at best, slim. Some find golf slightly less challenging to play than others, but ever since the very first ball was struck by a stick five centuries ago, no one has ever described it as an easy game to learn or has had the temerity to claim to have truly mastered it.

If it's any consolation to the hordes of hapless hackers throughout the world, there never will be perfect mastery. No matter how brilliantly you play a round, there's always a shot or two somewhere along the line that gets away. And that, as far as I'm concerned, explains the addictive pull of the game. Regardless of ability level, every player who steps onto the first tee never knows for sure whether he or she is about to spend the next few hours walking hand in hand with agony or ecstasy. Another thing I've learned is that no one enjoys being a loser. That does not mean golf should be taken in deadly earnest. Learning, practicing, and playing should be tackled with pleasure and enthusiasm—for once the game loses its feel-good factor, it ceases to be for amateurs the reason for its very existence.

The fact that you are reading this book suggests that you are already a fairly enthusiastic golfer or someone who is seriously

The effect of the path of the clubhead through the impact zone is explained in Fundamentals.

90

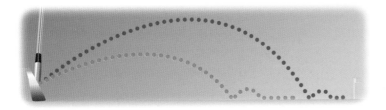

considering becoming one. The question this book poses is "how well, at this stage, do you really know the game?" Throughout this book you will be asked to test your knowledge on all areas of golf.

My accomplice is John Cook, winner of four European PGA events and now recognized as one of the leading teachers in the United Kingdom. He specializes in the short game, and is coach to the England national youth team. John is also Instruction Consultant to *Today's Golfer* magazine, Europe's top-selling sports publication. As the magazine's instruction editor, I have worked with John for several years and, like our readers, have become a great fan of his simple-to-digest and sound teaching methods.

Together, I think we have succeeded in covering virtually every aspect of golf in this book. And even if you find yourself struggling to answer the questions, you cannot fail to learn just by studying the correct answers, and the valuable instructional facts and golfing information they contain.

To discover whether you really do know the game, study your responses carefully before turning to the answers. Like the player aiming to sink a match-winning putt, you've got only one real chance.

Are you playing the correct clubs for your swing? Test your knowledge in the section on equipment.

David Ayres
Instruction Editor
Today's Golfer

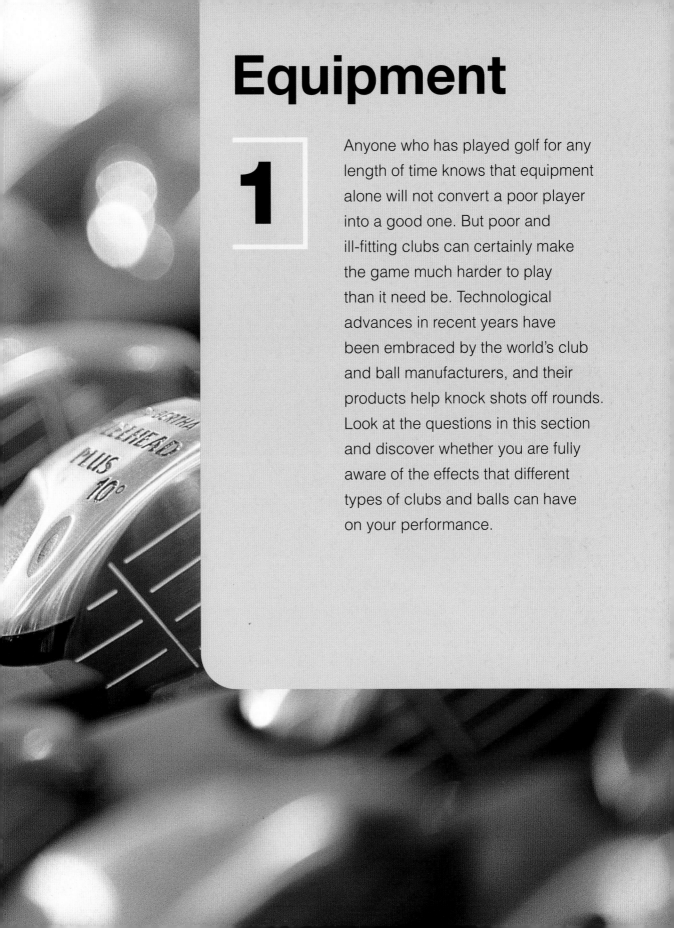

Equipment

1

Anyone who has played golf for any length of time knows that equipment alone will not convert a poor player into a good one. But poor and ill-fitting clubs can certainly make the game much harder to play than it need be. Technological advances in recent years have been embraced by the world's club and ball manufacturers, and their products help knock shots off rounds. Look at the questions in this section and discover whether you are fully aware of the effects that different types of clubs and balls can have on your performance.

Equipment

1.1

The most
important test

The most important test and valuable piece of advice on selecting golf clubs is "never buy until you try." It really doesn't matter how wonderful the equipment looks on the display stand in the pro shop—the vital test is how it performs in your hands.

You tend to push the ball out to the right on a fairly low trajectory. It is suggested that the grips fitted to your clubs could in some way be contributing to your unsatisfactory shot pattern. If the diagnosis is correct, they are likely to be:

A Too **thick** for your hands.

B Too **thin**.

C Made of **cheap plastic** rather than a good-quality rubber compound, causing the hands to slip open during the swing.

Q2
Titanium is the preferred choice of many leading manufacturers for the construction of metal clubheads, particularly drivers. What main advantage does the player gain from the use of this space age alloy?

A It is **harder** than other metals and therefore hits the ball further.

B It can be **worked** into more aerodynamically shaped clubheads.

C It is extremely **light**.

Q3 Why do players, particularly seniors, turn to the long putter for help when they develop the dreaded putting yips?

Q4 You buy a new set of irons but find that overall distances are down compared with your old set, trajectories are lower, and you fail to get as much stop on the ball when playing into greens. A friend (an experienced player and a low-handicapper) says you've chosen the wrong shafts. What is probably wrong with them?

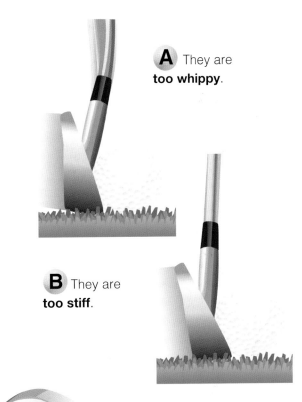

A They are **too whippy**.

B They are **too stiff**.

A Because it calls for a **split-handed** grip.

B It is easier to **aim**, and thus alleviates tension at address.

C The head is **heavier** and the player therefore has to swing it more slowly.

C Unlike previous clubs you have used, they are fitted **straight into the head** rather than via a hosel.

A perfect fit is when the fingernails of the top hand just touch the fleshy pad of the hand.

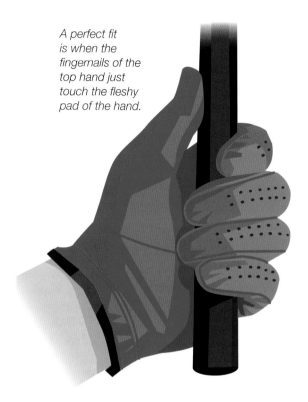

Answer: C

Although it conveniently happens to be harder than steel, the main benefit of titanium is its lightness, which allows manufacturers to create much larger heads without making them too heavy and therefore sacrificing swing speed. Because the clubface on a titanium driver is larger, the effective hitting area is increased, making it more forgiving and easier to use. Although some clubheads are as big as 400cc, anything larger is prone to suffer too much drag and turbulence through the air. The majority of leading manufacturers now think that a clubhead of 300cc to 360cc is about right.

Answer: A

Grips that are too large tend to restrict the necessary hand action and the release of the clubhead through the hitting zone, preventing the clubface from returning to square at impact. The result is a low fade or a push. Conversely, grips that are too thin usually promote overactive hands, causing the clubface to close through impact and result in the ball being drawn or pulled to the left. A perfect fit is when the fingernails of the top hand on the club just touch the fleshy pad at the base of the hand.

Titanium is popular with club manufacturers because the heads can be both large and light.

Separating the hands helps prevent the dreaded putting yips.

A3 Answer: A

The putting yips occur when the hands stop working together as a single unit on the handle and operate against each other through the impact zone, causing a wristy yip (or jerk) at the ball. Separating the hands—or even putting with just one hand on the club—prevents this from happening. And, as the long putter demands a split grip, it makes it virtually impossible to yip. Incidentally, a lot of people cannot understand why touring professionals are prone to attacks of the yips. The reason is simply because they are most likely to occur in high-pressure situations, and there are fewer high-pressure spots than the greens of a golf course when huge sums of money are riding on the putting skills of the players.

A4 Answer: B

The shot pattern is caused by the fact that the shafts in your clubs are too stiff for your swing speed and are therefore failing to deliver the necessary whip action at the bottom to propel the ball high and far. The lack of stop (or backspin) is another good indicator. Shafts that are too whippy will have the opposite effect, with the ball flying too high and hard to keep under control as far as accuracy is concerned. Shafts generally come in three main flexes—stiff (for players with powerful swings generating lots of clubhead speed), regular (suitable for most middle-of-the-road golfers), and whippy (for juniors, ladies, and seniors with slow swing speeds).

Experts agree that many players hinder themselves by using shafts that are too stiff for their particular swings. If you are in doubt about what type is suitable for you, ask a qualified professional at a nearby golf facility. He or she will be more than happy to offer you valuable advice and assistance.

The pattern of shots is greatly affected by the flex of the shaft.

Equipment

Learn the **tools** of the **trade**

Many novices and high-handicappers make the mistake of thinking that their bag of clubs is not complete unless it contains a driver. Most would see their strokes reduced if they left out the most difficult of all clubs to use.

Q6 A good golfing friend has bought you an expensive and unusual present—a hand-held electronic measuring device to determine yardages to the pin. Are you allowed to use it:

Q5 Some manufacturers incorporate tungsten and other heavy metal inserts and plugs in their clubheads (both woods and irons). Why?

A To provide **better weight** distribution.

B To establish a **lower center of gravity** to help the player get the ball into the air more easily.

C For better **feel**.

A **Whenever** you play?

B For **social rounds** only?

C During **official competition** rounds only?

Ratings are used by nearly all the leading manufacturers to identify the compression factor of their balls. Most are rated 80, 90, or 100. Who benefits most from the 100-compression models?

 When custom-fitting a new set of clubs, which measurement is most commonly used to determine the appropriate length of shaft for an individual?

A Senior players, ladies, and juniors with **slow swing speeds**.

B Those with **powerful** swings.

C Mr. and Mrs. **Average**.

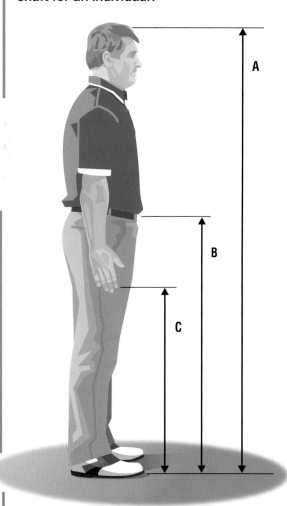

A The individual's overall **height**.

B The length of the individual's **legs**.

C The length of the individual's **fingertips** from the ground.

Metal plugs and inserts are used to improve the playability of woods and irons.

Answer: A B

A5

By using heavy metal plugs and inserts, clubmakers can concentrate weight where it will help make heads more forgiving on off-center shots and lower the center of gravity to get the ball airborne that much easier. Craftsmen of old would try to do exactly the same thing by boring holes in the soles of wooden heads and filling them with molten lead. Metal base plates served the same purpose. Thanks to computers, today's clubs are much better balanced and technically advanced than their historic predecessors.

Answer: B

A6

The use of electronic and other distance-measuring devices is strictly banned when it comes to competitions (unless the golf committee makes an exceptional rule). Caddies on the professional tours throughout the world very often use them before tournaments get officially underway to help them establish yardages to the pins from various locations. But the devices are left securely in the locker room and replaced by the caddy's notebook of yardages and other information once the competition officially begins.

Although useful, using distance-measuring devices during competitions is strictly forbidden.

Compression ratings do not refer to the hardness of the ball's cover, but how the whole ball compresses on the face of the club.

A8

Answer: C

The distance between the outstretched fingers of the hands (hanging naturally from the shoulders and down the sides of the body) is one of the most important factors when it comes to custom-fitting a set of clubs for an individual. Tall people often have long arms and their fingertips-to-ground measurement can be exactly the same as someone several inches shorter in overall height. Several other factors are obviously also taken into account by the fitter to determine a suitable set for an individual.

A7

Answer: B

Only players who generate a lot of power and clubhead speed can compress a 100-rated ball on the clubface sufficiently to get optimum performance from it. Most players will get the best results from a 90-compression ball, with slow swing-speed golfers (mainly juniors, seniors, and the majority of ladies) better served by one rated at 80 or even lower. Many golfers make the mistake of confusing compression with the hardness of a ball's cover. A hard compression (100) ball does not necessarily have a hard cover—in fact, many now have relatively soft outer covers for greater spin and better feel, particularly on short shots around the green.

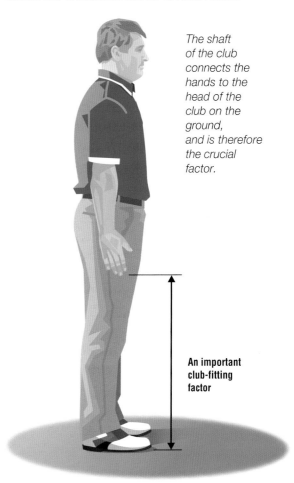

The shaft of the club connects the hands to the head of the club on the ground, and is therefore the crucial factor.

An important club-fitting factor

Give yourself a **sporting chance**

1.3

Most equipment experts agree that most players pay insufficient attention to the flex of their shaft and the condition and thickness of their grip. Get these two factors correct and you will give yourself a reasonable chance of playing well. Get them wrong and you have little chance of success.

Putters generally come in three head designs— heel-and-toe weighted, traditional blades, and mallets. What putting action is generally regarded as best suited to mallets?

Q9 **The sand traps at the course where you regularly play contain very light and fluffy sand. What type of wedge is best suited to get the ball out of the trap and onto the green?**

A A sand wedge with **plenty of bounce** built into the sole.

A The **rap** style.

B A sand wedge with **very little** bounce.

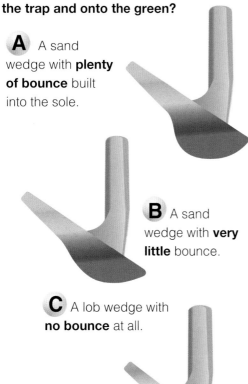

B The **low and slow** stroke.

C A lob wedge with **no bounce** at all.

C Wristy.

Although many amateurs play with graphite-shafted clubs, the vast majority of touring professionals prefer steel shafts (except for their drivers). Why?

Distance balls are rarely used by professional tour players and low-handicap players. This is generally because they:

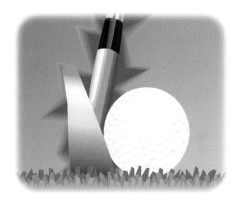

A Because steel shafts offer greater **consistency**.

A Lack **feel**.

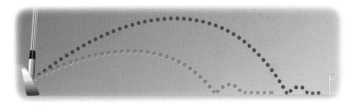

B Steel gives the player greater **distance**.

B Lack **height** when struck powerfully.

C Better **backspin** is achieved with steel shafts.

C Get **out of shape** too easily.

Bounce on a clubhead determines how deeply it digs into the sand.

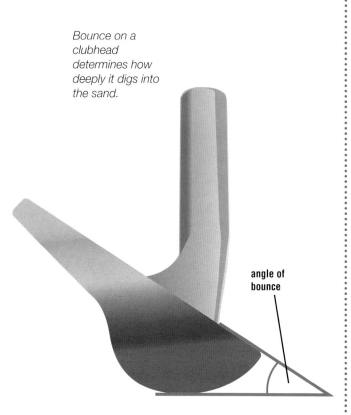

angle of
bounce

Answer: B

The mallet putter is designed mainly for the player who positions the ball well forward in the stance, takes the club back slowly and low to the ground, and tends to hit the ball slightly on the upswing, causing it to roll with plenty of topspin to the hole. The other types of putters are best suited to players who rap their putts. These golfers stand with their weight slightly on the left foot and are inclined to pick the head of the club up steeper and accelerate hard through the ball with a restricted follow-through. Establish what action you use and you are on the way to finding the type of putter to suit your style.

Answer: A

Plenty of bounce (at least 11 degrees) is needed to prevent a sand wedge from burying itself too deeply into light and fluffy sand and failing to extricate the ball. Sand or lob wedges with little or no bounce are therefore completely unsuitable for this type of sand. A ball sitting on wet or hard sand demands an entirely different club. One with bounce would skid off the sand and the leading edge would strike the ball in its center, sending it into the lip or low out of the sand with no control whatsoever, so you would probably reach for your pitching wedge to play this shot.

Mallet putters are heavier than conventional putters, and may be preferred by players who like to position the ball forward in their stance.

Answer: A

It's a fact that, with a very few exceptions, nearly all the world's leading professionals have steel shafts fitted to all their clubs other than to their drivers. Steel is accepted as offering greater consistency in both length and dispersion than graphite, and it is exactly that feature the pros are seeking in their clubs. When it comes to their drivers (and if the course they are playing happens to have fairly wide fairways), they are sometimes prepared to sacrifice a little accuracy for raw power. The majority of amateurs have a different outlook. They are constantly seeking extra yards, hence many have switched to graphite shafts in recent years.

Steel is regarded as being the best bet for consistency.

Graphite will often provide extra yardage.

Answer: A

Because they can hit the ball such massive distances at will, most good players seek the quality of feel when selecting a ball. Around the greens, particularly, they like to feel the ball on the clubface when they play a shot—and that is hard to attain with a distance ball, many of which have hard outer covers and tend to fly off the face much faster than their soft-cover cousins. Incidentally, as far as backspin is concerned, many of the new generation distance balls now boast the same spin rate as the softer-covered balls.

The feel off the clubface is vital to professionals and low-handicappers, as it provides valuable feedback on ball striking.

Equipment

1.4 Choose the **right putter**

The most frequently used club in the bag is the putter, being called upon at least 36 times by most amateurs during a normal round of golf. That's why the purchase of a putter should warrant more consideration than any other piece of equipment.

Q14 The heels of your irons usually strike the ground first at impact, causing you to pull shots to the left of where you want the ball to go. The lie of the club (the angle at which the sole sits on the ground) is:

A Too **upright**.

Q13 In addition to its lightness and claims that it generates more clubhead speed, graphite is also chosen by some players for one other reason. What is that?

A It absorbs vibration, helping **prevent injuries** to the hands and wrists.

B Too **flat**.

B It helps get the ball **into the air** more easily.

C It enables players to achieve more **accuracy** with their shots.

 Many game-improvement clubs (woods and irons) feature offset heads, where the leading edge of the clubhead is effectively set back from the front of the hosel. What main benefit does this design offer the high-handicapper?

A It helps create more **clubhead speed** and therefore greater distance.

B It gives greater **accuracy**.

C It helps players get the ball **into the air** more easily.

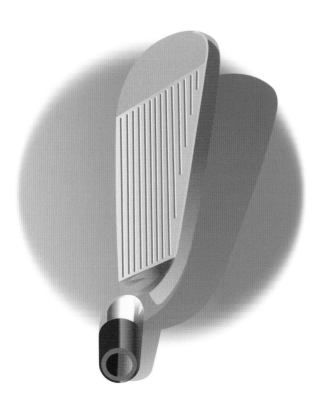

Why are balls that generate a lot of backspin (desirable for stopping the ball quickly on greens) not usually suitable for the less-accomplished player?

A They are generally well **down on distance**.

B They also produce a **lot of sidespin**.

C Because of their composition, they are easily **blown off line** in windy conditions.

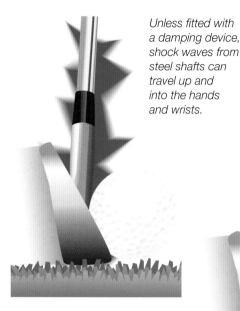

Unless fitted with a damping device, shock waves from steel shafts can travel up and into the hands and wrists.

Graphite shafts tend to absorb most of the shock waves.

A14 Answer: A

A club that is too upright for the player will result in the heel of the head coming into contact first with the turf, causing the face to close and the ball to be pulled to the left of target. If the lie is correct, the toe should actually sit slightly off the ground at address to compensate for the bowing effect of the shaft downward during the swing. Contrary to popular belief, the height of a player does not necessarily affect the lie angle of his or her clubs. The overall length of a club and its position at impact are the main determining factors the experts take into consideration.

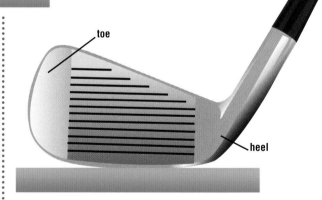

toe

heel

There needs to be a little space between the toe and the ground to allow for the bowing effect of the shaft during the swing.

A13 Answer: A

A series of shock waves travel up the shaft and into the hands when impact between clubhead and ball takes place, and graphite generally tends to absorb these waves better than steel. Seniors or others who have arthritis, or those with past injuries to their wrists or elbows, can benefit by using graphite shafts in their clubs. It should be noted that grips also have a bearing on shock absorption and that many steel shafts also now come with built-in dampers to reduce shock.

Answer: C

By incorporating offset into the design of a club, the manufacturers are moving the center of gravity back from the center of the shaft, which results in the ball launching higher and with added backspin for a higher flight path. Most of today's game improvement clubs are designed with offset, whereas traditional sets of blade-type irons have little or none. It is also a fact that clubs with increased offset produce a right-to-left ball flight. They can therefore help the majority of high-handicap players who are usually fighting a slice.

Answer: B

A ball either spins a lot or it doesn't. There's no such thing (at least, not at the time of writing) as a ball that will spin in one plane but not the other. So, if a ball produces the necessary spin required to make it stop quickly on the greens, it will also be more prone to slice or draw if clubhead contact is not square and traveling along the correct path through the hitting zone. Before you rush out and buy a sleeve of balls that offer pro backspin, think of where it might land well before the green actually comes into play!

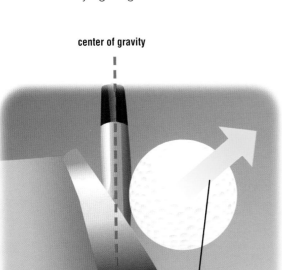

center of gravity

higher flight path

Most of today's game improvement clubs have offset heads.

Remember that high-spin balls are more likely to slice or hook.

Fundamentals

Look closely at the top players in the world. Despite their physical differences and the idiosyncrasies of their respective swings, they all have one thing in common—a full understanding and mastery of what are commonly known as the *fundamentals*. Grip, stance and aim, posture, and basic swing factors are the foundations on which good golf is built. Study, learn, and master them, and you will never again have to walk a course hand in hand with frustration and misery. So just how familiar are you with the golden basics of the game? This section will help you find out.

2.1

Lay **solid foundations**

It is impossible to over-emphasize the importance of the four fundamentals: grip, aim, stance, and posture. If you get them right, you will be well on the way to becoming a successful golfer.

Q1 The "V"s formed between the forefinger and thumb on each hand are often referred to and given as reference points when the conventional grip is being taught and discussed. As far as a right-hander is concerned, at address, the Vs should point:

A Straight at the **chin**.

B Between the chin and **left** shoulder.

C Between the chin and **right** shoulder.

Q2 Which of the following swing path patterns through the hitting zone is recognized as the one that, coupled with certain grip and stance factors, produces a hook (right-to-left flight on the ball)?

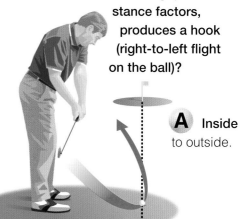

A Inside to outside.

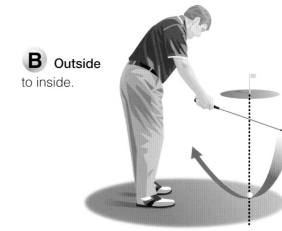

B Outside to inside.

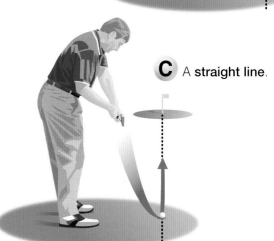

C A straight line.

Q3 The halfway back position (arms parallel to the ground) provides a valuable checkpoint as to whether the clubhead has been taken away square to the target line. Where should the toe of the clubhead be pointing at this stage of the swing?

A Toward the **sky**.

B Toward the **front**.

C Toward the **back**.

Q4 One of the questions asked most often by newcomers to the game is, "How far do I stand from the ball at address for normal shots?" Measuring between the butt end of the club and the top of the thigh, it should be:

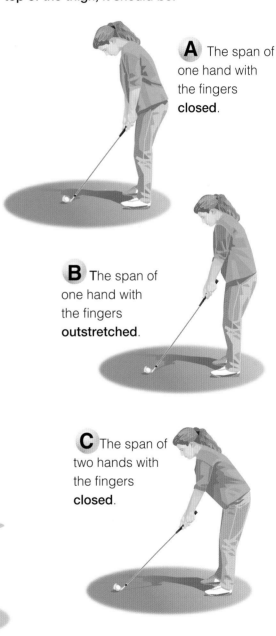

A The span of one hand with the fingers **closed**.

B The span of one hand with the fingers **outstretched**.

C The span of two hands with the fingers **closed**.

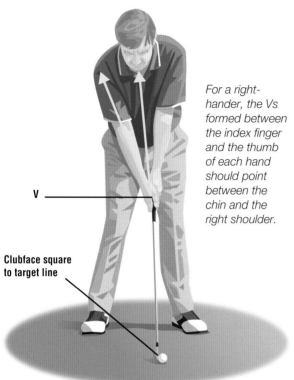

For a right-hander, the Vs formed between the index finger and the thumb of each hand should point between the chin and the right shoulder.

V

Clubface square to target line

Answer: **A**

An inside-to-outside path by the clubhead through the hitting zone, generally coupled with a strong grip and a closed stance, will produce a counterclockwise spin on the ball, causing it to hook and move from right to left through the air. Most novices and high-handicappers attack the ball on an out-to-in path, causing the ball to slice on a left-to-right path. This usually results in loss of potential distance. The path required to hit the ball straight is from the inside of the line to square at impact and then back inside.

A hook is achieved with an inside-to-outside clubhead path through the hitting zone.

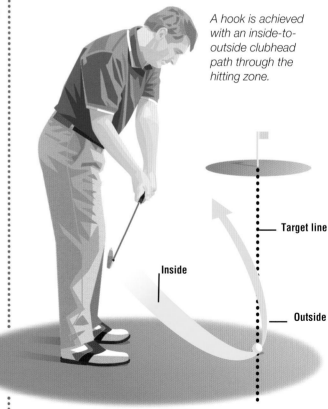

Target line

Inside

Outside

Answer: **C**

When looking down on the hands at address, the Vs formed between the index finger and thumb of both hands should point between the chin and right shoulder to ensure that the clubface is returned to the ball square to the target line. Grips where the Vs point straight to the chin, or between the chin and left shoulder, are referred to as "weak" grips and return the clubface to the ball in an open position (pointing right of the target line). Conversely, the clubhead will return to impact closed (pointing left of the target line) if the Vs point beyond the right shoulder.

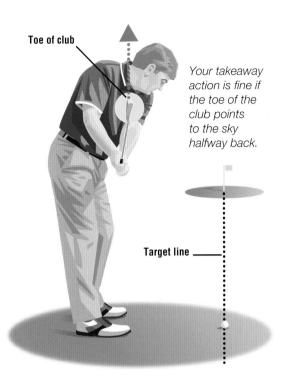

Toe of club

Your takeaway action is fine if the toe of the club points to the sky halfway back.

Target line

A4 **Answer: B**

The general rule of how far you should stand from the ball at address is one hand with outstretched fingers between the butt end of the club and the thigh. It's virtually impossible to make a solid contact with the ball if you stand too near to it or too far away. Too near usually results in an excessively upright swing and too steep an angle of attack into the ball; too far demands a very flat swing and a slice-inducing out-to-in swing path through the hitting zone.

How far you stand from the ball at address is critical.

A3 **Answer: A**

The toe of the club should be pointing straight up to the sky if it has been taken away squarely, and therefore correctly, from the ball. If it is pointing toward the target, it means that it has been taken away closed and will almost certainly result in the ball being hooked or pulled to the left. Pointing away from the target is good evidence that the wrists have fanned the clubface open. The likely outcome is a slice or a weak push to the right of the intended target.

A good guide as to how far you should stand from the ball is one hand with outstretched fingers between the butt end of the club and the thigh.

The Fundamentals

2.2

Don't neglect **your grip**

The grip is arguably the most important of the fundamentals —and probably the most neglected. A correct grip will ensure the clubhead is returned to the ball squarely to the target line. A bad one often sparks a chain reaction of swing faults.

How far apart you place your feet at address is critical when it comes to overall balance, and can therefore have a big bearing on how you hit the ball. What width is generally regarded as ideal for normal full shots?

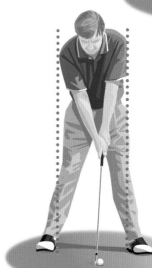

A **Less** than the width of the shoulders.

B The **width** of the shoulders.

C A little **wider** than the shoulders.

Q5 You are often guilty of striking the top of the ball or thinning it when playing irons. Looking at your ball position at address as one of the possible causes, it is likely to be:

A Too near the **back** foot.

B Too near the **front** foot.

Q7 Much is mentioned about the top of the swing and where the clubhead and shaft should be pointing. But when is the backswing generally regarded as being complete?

A When your club is at least **parallel** to the ground.

B When you can't get the clubhead back **any further.**

C When your **left shoulder** is pointing at the ball.

Q8 Ask most teachers for a list of swing problems as far as high-handicappers are concerned and you can safely bet that incorrect grip pressure will feature pretty high up. Based on a scale of one to ten (with one being the lightest and ten the tightest), how tightly should the handle be gripped for normal shots?

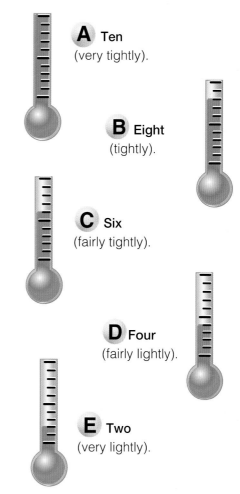

A Ten (very tightly).

B Eight (tightly).

C Six (fairly tightly).

D Four (fairly lightly).

E Two (very lightly).

33

Do not position the ball too far forward in the stance at address, as it will result in you "topping" the ball.

Hitting top of the ball

Base of the swing arc

Answer: B

A6

The width of the shoulders is correct for normal full shots, but remember that this width relates to the heels rather than the out-turned toes, usually a difference of several inches. It's surprising how many players use their out-turned toes to fix the width, resulting in a narrow stance where the legs are unable to resist the turning of the upper body. It also causes excessive lateral body movement and poor balance. Although placing the heels wider than shoulder width apart gives a solid feeling at address, it actually restricts the amount of hip and body turn and therefore results in a loss of potential power.

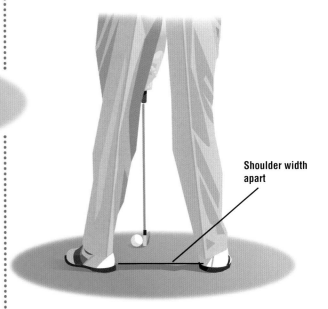

Shoulder width apart

The heels of the feet should be shoulder width apart for normal full shots.

Answer: B

A5

In an effort to get the ball into the air, many players —particularly high-handicappers—position the ball too far forward in their stance, in the belief they are adding effective loft to the clubface at impact. All they actually succeed in doing is to strike the top of the ball as the club moves from its lowest point in the downswing (the base of the swing arc) and starts to rise in the upswing.

Answer: C

The position of the clubhead at the top of the swing varies from player to player, depending on age and physical condition. Many players make the mistake of trying to get the club too far back, the main results being excessive lateral body movement, loss of rhythm and tempo, and a loosening of the grip. The only real checkpoint is the left shoulder. When it is pointing at the ball, you have completed your backswing.

Top of swing

The left shoulder is a good guide as to how far back you should swing the club.

Answer: D

All the top tour players agree that the vast majority of amateurs grip the club far too tightly, causing unwanted tension in their muscles and making it virtually impossible to attain a fluid and relaxed swing. On a scale of one to ten, your grip pressure should be about four.

Four out of ten

The pressure of your grip should be fairly light

On a scale of one to ten, grip pressure should be about four— about the same strength as you would use to squeeze a toothpaste tube or hold a small bird in your hand.

Holding a bird

Squeezing a toothpaste tube

The Fundamentals

2.3 Take **aim** for **success**

Aiming the ball carefully at the target is crucial. Get it wrong and the only way to hit the ball on line is to compensate by making an incorrect swing. Top players never hit a shot until they are certain their clubhead is positioned correctly behind the ball.

Q9 Your ball has come to rest on a fairly steep slope and will be higher than your feet when you play your next shot. What flight pattern do you expect the ball to take?

A High. **B** Low.

C Left to right. **D** Right to left.

Q10 Many teachers recommend that the back foot be turned in toward the target to help cure a particularly common swing fault. This fault is:

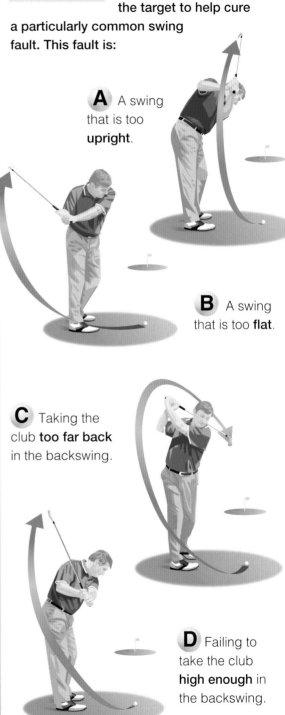

A A swing that is too **upright**.

B A swing that is too **flat**.

C Taking the club **too far back** in the backswing.

D Failing to take the club **high enough** in the backswing.

Q11 Players who habitually slice the ball on a left-to-right flight path often do so because they fail to position the ball correctly at address. They are likely to have it:

A Too far **ahead** of center.

B Too far **behind** center.

Q12 Nearly all the professional tour players "waggle" the clubhead backward and forward over the ball before starting their swing. What main advantage do they gain from this maneuver?

A The chance to check their **grip** is secure.

B Being able to **fix the path** of their takeaway.

C The **easing of tension** in the hands, arms, and shoulders.

The flight of the ball will automatically be right to left.

 **Answer: C**

Turning the back foot in toward the target at address and keeping it there during the swing is a well-proven cure for those who tend to overswing the club in the backswing. Placed in this position, the foot and lower leg restrict the turning motion of the hips and shoulders and help prevent the club from being taken beyond parallel at the top. Some players use this setup to restrict their action when called upon to play shots demanding less than a full swing with a particular club.

 Answer: D

When the ball is played from a position higher than the feet it will automatically fly on a right-to-left path. Because this is the most powerful of all flight patterns, the best thing to do is to take less club than normal for the distance required and to counteract the natural flight path by aiming to the right of the target. Other things to remember when playing this shot are to grip down the handle to effectively shorten the club and stand a little more upright than your normal address posture.

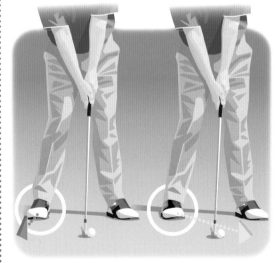

Turning the back foot in toward the target helps to prevent overswinging the club in the backswing.

The further forward the ball is placed at address increases the chances of a slice.

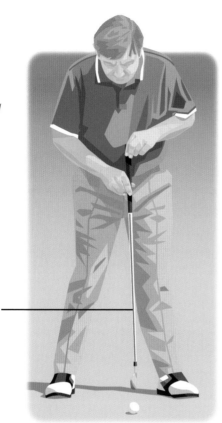

Check ball position at address with a club.

A12

Answer: C

Waggling the club before starting the swing is a wonderful way of ridding yourself of the biggest threat to a smooth, free-flowing swing—tension in the hands, arms, and shoulders. There are no set rules as far as waggling is concerned. Some players pass the clubhead back and forward over the ball once only, and others carry out the exercise several times before starting the actual swing. The vast majority of high-handicappers who make the big mistake of snatching the clubhead back too fast from the ball at address are well advised to make two or three slow and deliberate waggles ahead of the real swing. They will discover it helps them achieve a far more balanced and successful low 'n' slow start.

A11

Answer: A

Having the ball too far ahead in the stance means that the clubhead will almost certainly be traveling from out to in at impact. And, coupled with an open clubface, that is a surefire recipe for a distance-robbing, left-to-right slice. The furthest forward the ball should be at address is opposite the front heel when playing the driver. Even then, extra care has to be taken to ensure that the ball position does not pull the shoulders open to create an out-to-in path through the hitting zone. Nearly all fairway wood and iron shots are played with the ball positioned between the inside of the front heel and the center of the stance.

Tension at address (above left) is a real swing killer and can be eliminated by waggling the club before starting the swing.

2.4

Set up correctly

Adopting the correct stance and posture will ensure that the ball is positioned in the right spot between the feet at address. This means that the player is set up to make a smooth and well-balanced swing, sending the ball flying toward its target.

Q13

Correct alignment for straight shots calls for the feet, hips, and shoulders all to be aimed parallel to the intended target line. As far as gripping the club is concerned, should it be completed:

A **Before** taking up the address position?

B **After** making sure your feet, hips, and shoulders are in the correct position?

C By placing one hand on the grip, checking that the leading edge of the face is **square to the target**, and then adding the other hand?

Q14

The smooth and correct transition from backswing to downswing is one of the keys to a smooth and powerful path through the hitting area. Once the top-of-the-swing position has been reached, what is the key move to initiate the downswing?

A Moving the weight onto the **left side**.

B **Turning** the shoulders toward the target.

C Moving the **hips down**.

Q15 The plane on which the club is swung is critical. Swinging too shallow leads to a flat and out-to-in action through impact, and too upright results in a much too steep angle of attack into the ball. As a checkpoint, where should the butt end of the club be pointing when the left arm (for right-handers) is parallel with the ground during the downswing?

Q16 Good players can often be seen carrying out a practice drill where they push the butt end of their driver lightly into their navel, grip down the shaft, and swing the club backward and forward. What is the object of the exercise?

A Inside the ball.

B Outside the ball.

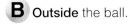

C At the ball.

A To check **how far** they are standing from the ball.

B To check that the grip **remains square** as the arms move away.

C To check whether their overall **takeaway** is correct.

A14

Moving the weight onto the left side is the correct way to make the transition from backswing to downswing. The uncoiling of the left side will then pull the arms down and ensure an in-to-square-to-in clubhead path through the hitting area. Poor players often make the big mistake of starting the backswing by turning their shoulders. This results in what is called a casting action of the arms (because of its similarity to casting a fishing rod) and a slice-inducing out-to-in clubhead path through impact.

Establish your grip before you place the clubhead on the ground.

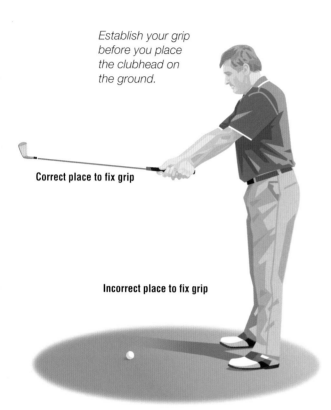

Correct place to fix grip

Incorrect place to fix grip

A13

Answer: A

The correct time to establish your grip on the club is before you place the clubhead behind the ball and align yourself square to the target. Placing the clubhead behind the ball at address and then adjusting your grip often results in the clubface being twisted off line as the grip is taken up. It is then normally returned either left or right of target through the hitting area.

Start the downswing by moving your weight onto the left side.

Answer: C

As a rough guide to finding the correct swing plane, the butt end of the grip should point at the ball when the left arm (for right-handers) is parallel with the ground in the downswing. If it points well inside the ball, the plane is too upright and will result in a tilting action of the body, rather than a turn, and too steep an angle into the ball at impact. Players whose swing planes are too flat will find the butt end of the grip will point outside the ball. Their action will be flat and will usually result in an out-to-in slicing path through the hitting zone.

Arm parallel to ground

Here's a simple way of determining your correct swing plane.

Butt end of grip

Try this drill for a synchronized takeaway.

Answer: C

Keeping the arms and body synchronized as you take the clubhead away from the ball is of paramount importance. An excellent drill made popular by David Leadbetter and Nick Faldo is to adopt your normal stance, rest the butt end of your driver in the navel, grip down the shaft, and then start the club back. Keeping the butt end in the navel ensures that the arm swing and the body turn are in unison. Now all you have to do is adopt the same synchronized takeaway in your real play.

43

3

The Long/Mid Game

As far as a golfer is concerned, few sights are more welcome than that of a ball whizzing off the face of a wood or long iron, soaring into the blue sky, and coming to rest either in the middle of a fairway or a green —with the proviso, of course, that it's off their club rather than that of their opponent! A good long game is, without a doubt, what all golfers aspire to. But it's an area where technique and knowledge always prove the victors over brute force. Check out in this section whether ignorance is costing you valuable yards and accuracy on the course.

3.1 The smooth route to **distance**

The vast majority of players who experience trouble with their long game are guilty of trying to hit at the ball instead of smoothly swinging the clubhead through it. Distance comes from correct fundamentals and technique—not from force.

Q1 **Your efforts with a driver are not very successful, with the ball normally slicing from left to right and robbing you of valuable distance. The height at which the ball is teed up can have a bearing on the shape of a shot. To solve your particular problem, you should consider:**

A Teeing it **higher**.

B Teeing it **lower**.

C **Not using** a tee at all.

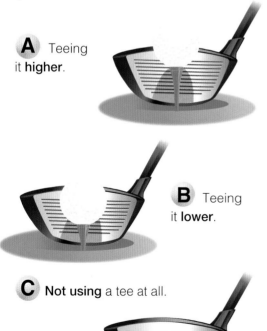

Q2 **It is generally assumed that the toes of the front foot should be splayed toward the target at address. So where should the ball be positioned for maximum distance when playing a driver?**

A Opposite the **front toes**.

B Opposite the **front heel**.

C Just **forward** of center.

D **Center** of the stance.

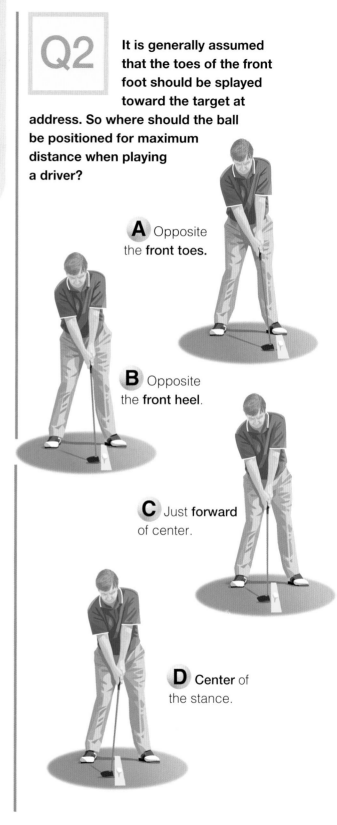

Q3 Wanting to take full advantage of the wide and bone-dry fairways of the course you are playing, what can you do to generate extra roll on the ball and therefore gain additional overall distance on your shots?

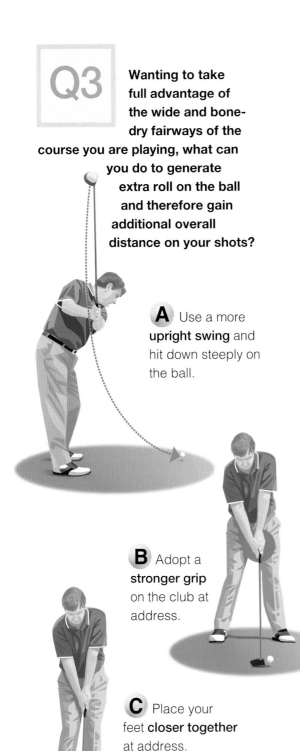

A Use a more **upright swing** and hit down steeply on the ball.

B Adopt a **stronger grip** on the club at address.

C Place your feet **closer together** at address.

Q4 Although quite difficult and not advised for novices and high-handicappers, it is sometimes very useful on long holes to be able to use the driver when the ball is sitting on the fairway. Which three of the following six points should be observed to ensure success?

A Grip the club a little **tighter** than normal at address.

B Grip the club **lightly** at address.

C Position the ball the same as when **playing off a tee**.

D Position the ball a **little further back** than when playing the ball from off a tee.

E Keep the weight **evenly distributed** on both feet through impact.

F **Transfer** the body weight to the front foot through impact.

47

Answer: A

Teeing the ball too low (below the height of the top of the face of the driver) nearly always promotes a steep angle of attack into the ball on an out-to-in swing path, imparting slice spin and causing the ball to slide from left to right. Nearly all good players tee the ball well above the height of the clubhead to encourage a square-to-square path through the impact zone and a little draw spin, which results in the ball rolling more on landing.

Teeing the ball high encourages draw spin and helps prevent an excessively steep angle of attack into the ball.

The ball should be positioned just opposite the heel of the front foot at address for maximum distance.

Front heel

Angle of attack is too steep

Answer: B

The driver from a tee is the only shot in golf where the ball is struck when the clubhead has gone beyond the base of its downward arc and is just beginning to rise into the follow-through. This calls for the ball to be positioned at address opposite the heel of the front foot. The most common mistake is to have the ball too far forward at address, which can result in the shoulders being drawn open and an out-to-in clubhead path at impact. Positioning the ball too far back in the stance results in an unwanted steep angle of attack into the ball and, more often than not, a chopping action under it.

A strong grip, with at least three knuckles of the left hand showing at address, helps to add run to the ball.

A3 **Answer: B**

Taking a stronger grip on the club so that, for right-handers, at least three knuckles of the left hand can be seen at address, reduces the effective loft of the club at impact and helps promote a hooking (right-to-left) flight pattern. This is what you are seeking on a long hole in dry conditions —provided, of course, the fairway is wide enough to accommodate the flight path and increased run on the ball. Don't confuse the term stronger grip with tighter grip. All that a stronger grip means is turning the hands on the handle more toward the back shoulder.

A4 **Answer: B C & F**

Players are not often called upon to use a driver to play a ball sitting on a fairway. Although novices and high-handicappers are advised to leave well enough alone, the more competent shouldn't be afraid of the shot, provided they observe at least three simple points. First of all, don't allow tension to take control and result in your gripping the club tighter than you normally do. Secondly, position the ball at address exactly the same as when it's on a tee (opposite the heel of the front foot). Then, take your normal swing and concentrate on transferring the body weight to the front foot through the impact zone to prevent scooping the ball into the air.

Follow three golden rules and you'll be able to use your driver from the fairway.

3.2

Make it easy
on yourself

Several options are usually available when long shots are necessary during play. Always select a club you are confident that you can perform well with, rather than hope for a lifetime's best hit with a more difficult one.

When in a competitive situation and faced with long shots (mainly in excess of 175 yards) to greens from fairways, novices and high-handicappers are best advised to use:

A A fairway wood.

Q5 Releasing the clubhead through the impact zone is the way in which clubhead speed—and therefore distance—is obtained. Which of the following swing throughs helps right-handed players to release correctly?

A Increase space between forearms through impact.

B Maintain address position of forearms through impact.

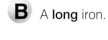

B A **long** iron.

C Have **right forearm** touch left forearm through impact.

Q7 The knee of the back leg has an important role to play in the golf swing. It should be flexed at address and to the top of the backswing, but what should happen to it at the start of the downswing?

Q8 Lifting the front heel during the backswing and keeping it raised until the start of the downswing is recommended for particular players. Which?

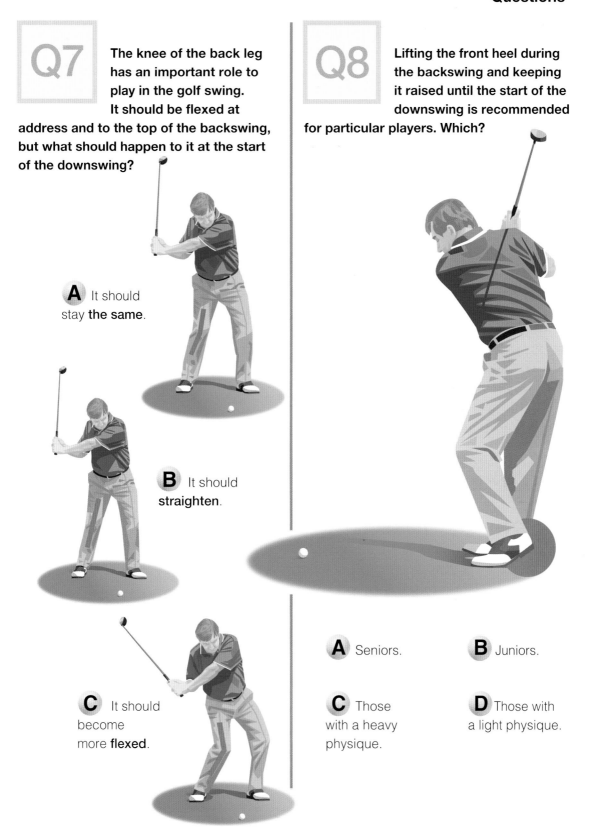

A It should stay **the same**.

B It should **straighten**.

C It should become more **flexed**.

A Seniors.

B Juniors.

C Those with a heavy physique.

D Those with a light physique.

Proper release of the clubhead through impact helps to send the ball a long way.

Answer: A

A6 In addition to the driver, long irons are generally regarded as the most difficult clubs in the bag to use. So, in competitive situations, novices and high-handicappers are best advised to reach for a fairway wood. In addition to possessing more loft, the soles of fairway woods are generally much more forgiving than those of long irons. When the result of the shot is unimportant, players should use every opportunity to improve their long-iron skills, because fairway woods are not suitable in windy conditions.

The fairway wood is a safer option than the long iron for most club players.

Answer: C

A5 Thinking of touching your left forearm with the right forearm through impact is an excellent way to help players release the clubhead correctly to generate maximum clubhead speed and, therefore, distance. Failure to release the club results in the forearms remaining apart and, very often, the face of the club pointing toward the sky in the first half of the follow-through.

Correct flexing of the right knee helps to achieve a good swing.

Retain flex here during the swing.

Answer: A

A7

Establishing flex in the back knee from address until the top of the backswing helps the legs to resist the turning motion of the upper body to create a powerful coil, prevents unwanted lateral movement, and helps ensure that there is no overswing. The flex is then maintained well into the downswing to prevent the path of the swing from becoming too steep into the ball and the clubhead chopping under it. A straight and stiff back leg at any time during the swing should be avoided as it leads to a multitude of bad shots.

Answer: A & C

A8

Lifting the front heel during the backswing helps those whose bodies are not particularly flexible to make a better body turn. It is therefore a useful technique for seniors and those with a heavy physique. Once the top of the backswing has been attained, the heel should be returned to the ground to help initiate the downswing. This will help to get the weight moving in the right direction—toward your target.

Lifting the front heel during the backswing helps promote a better body turn.

Raise heel

It should then return to the ground to initiate the downswing.

Then return it

3.3

Create a **coil for power**

Distance hitting is achieved through the powerful coil effect created by the legs and lower body resisting the turning motion of the upper body. This results in the hips turning by about 45 degrees, compared with the 90-degree turn of the shoulders.

Q10

Players with fairly low swing speeds are often advised to use a 3 wood for their tee shots rather than a driver. This is because:

A The 3 wood is designed for **low swing speeds**.

Q9

If you usually swing a full wedge at 75 percent of your full potential strength or speed, what percentage should you employ for your driver?

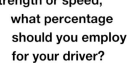

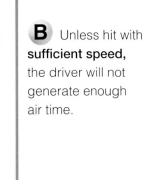

A 85 percent.

B 75 percent.

C 65 percent.

B Unless hit with **sufficient speed,** the driver will not generate enough air time.

C Slow swingers might as well take the **easier-to-hit 3 wood** because, even with a driver, they can't normally reach par fours in the regulation two shots.

Q11

Your ball has come to rest in a sand trap about 180 yards from the green. It is sitting nicely on top of the sand and there is no lip to clear at the front. Deciding to "have a go" with a fairway wood, you should at address:

A **Shuffle** your feet until they are well down in the sand.

B **Shuffle** feet lightly in the sand.

Q12

At what stage of the swing should the wrists uncock to produce maximum clubhead speed at impact?

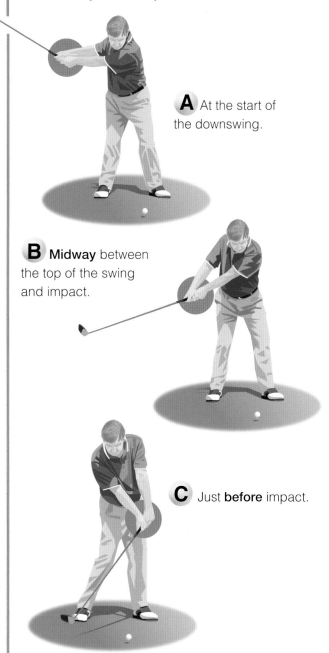

A At the start of the downswing.

B **Midway** between the top of the swing and impact.

C Just **before** impact.

All the top stars swing each of their clubs with exactly the same tempo. That's why they are such consistent performers.

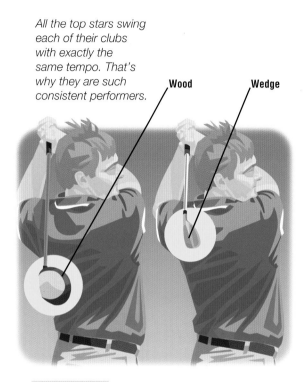

Wood

Wedge

Answer: B

A 10

It is wrong for all golfers to automatically assume that the driver will give them maximum length off the tee. Because of its straight face, the driver needs to be struck at sufficient speed to allow it to get the ball airborne and stay there for long enough to cover plenty of distance. The 3 wood, with its increased clubhead loft, does not need as much speed at impact to achieve satisfactory liftoff, trajectory, and air time. It is therefore a much better choice for those who do not generate much clubhead speed.

A9 # Answer: B

Most high-handicappers make the big mistake of trying to hit their woods and long irons harder than their wedges because the ball has further to travel. Watch the top touring stars and you will discover that virtually all of them swing each club with exactly the same tempo, allowing the combination of longer shaft and less clubhead loft to produce the required yardage. Many top teachers recommend that students imagine they are hitting a three-quarter wedge shot when they play their drivers and other long clubs.

3 wood

Driver

The 3 wood is much better than a driver off the tee for those who do not generate much clubhead speed.

A11 Answer: B

One of the keys to success when hitting a fairway wood or long iron from sand is to achieve a clean contact with the ball. Nestling the feet well down into the sand will increase the likelihood of making contact with the sand before the ball, and will rob the clubhead of some of its speed. It is better to shuffle the feet lightly into the sand, making sure they have enough grip to retain balance throughout the swing.

Don't dig the feet too deeply into the sand when hitting long irons or fairway woods from fairway bunkers.

A12 Answer: C

Maximum clubhead speed, and therefore distance, is achieved by uncocking the wrists as late as possible in the swing—ideally, just before impact. The angle between the wrists and the shaft of the club at the top of the swing (normally about 90 degrees) should be maintained until the arms are at least parallel with the ground on the way down. The wrists should then be uncocked as the clubhead enters the impact zone to unleash maximum clubhead speed. A useful way of working on the late uncocking of the wrists is to swing a club without striking a ball and to try to delay the "swish" noise of the shaft and clubhead until just before the hitting zone.

Release wrists here

A late release of the wrists helps maximize clubhead speed at impact and distance.

57

4

The Short Game

Ask virtually any club or touring professional how the average high-handicap club golfer can achieve better scores, and they will tell you that the answer lies in the short game. Few golfers bother to practice and improve their putting and greenside skills, yet it is here that bogeys and double bogeys can be converted into pars and even birdies by those who can never hope (or have the time) to achieve the power and long-shot accuracy of the game's elite. Test your short-game knowledge and learn from studying this important section. Without realizing it, you will almost certainly be taking a painless route to a lower handicap.

4.1

Why **handicaps** are high

At least 70 percent of shots played during a normal round of golf are from within 100 yards of the pin. Yet, most players who make the effort to practice devote only about 10 percent of their time to this section of the game.

Q2 Your ball comes to rest on cut grass 10 yards from the green and just in front of a deep sand trap with a fairly steep lip. You now need to play a cut shot over the sand trap and stop the ball quickly on the green. You should set up:

A With your shoulders, hips, feet, and the clubface **square** to the pin.

Q1 Why do many of the top stars hover their putters just above the ground at address rather than rest them on the grass immediately behind the ball before making their stroke?

A To help them **stand tall** through the stroke.

B So they can see the exact **location** of the center of the blade more easily .

B With your shoulders, hips, and feet aiming **a little left** of the pin but with the clubface square to it.

C To help them achieve a **smooth takeaway**.

C With your shoulders, hips, and feet pointing **right of the pin** but the clubface open to it.

Q3 Your ball has come to rest on the second cut around the green but hard up against the collar of the longer grass. Several options are open to you, including what has commonly become known in recent years as the bellied-wedge shot. What does this entail?

 Q4 Players with a particular greenside chipping problem are recommended by their teachers to practice with a ball or the shaft of a club placed under the outside edge of their back foot. What does this help them achieve?

A Using the underside of a **lofted wood** to move it forward with topspin.

A Correct **weight** distribution.

B Hitting it on the top with **an iron** to make it jump up and onto the green.

B The required **takeaway** path from the ball.

C Hitting the equator (center) of the ball with the leading edge of a **lofted club**.

C Correct hip and shoulder **angle**.

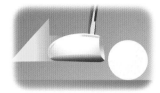

*Hovering the head
of the putter at
address will
reduce tension.*

Answer: **B**

A2

The necessary result is
achieved by setting up with
your shoulders, hips, and feet
all facing a little left of the target but with
the leading edge of the clubface pointing
straight at it. Simply swinging along the line
of your feet will create an out-to-in swing path
and result in the clubface cutting the ball up
high with lots of backspin to help it stop
quickly on landing.

Answer: **C**

A1

A smooth stroke is absolutely
essential for successful
putting and cannot be
achieved with a disjointed and jerky
takeaway. Hovering the head of the putter
just above the ground when addressing the
ball helps to eliminate tension, create a
smooth action, and prevent the head from
making contact with the ground and
deflecting it as it starts back.

*Set up correctly
and watch the
ball fly toward
the target.*

Answer: **C**

Lee Trevino is credited with solving the tricky problem of how to successfully play a ball sitting hard against a collar of longer grass. Using a sand wedge, he simply hovers the clubhead above the ground and strikes the middle of the ball—the "belly"—with the leading edge of the club, causing it to run low to the green. So, this shot became known as the bellied wedge.

Strike the "belly" of the ball with the leading edge of a lofted club.

Answer: **A**

One of the essentials of good chipping is setting the weight on the front foot at address and keeping it there throughout the shot. Placing a ball or the shaft under the outside of the back foot automatically places the body weight where it needs to be. Some teachers go even further by asking pupils to practice hitting chip shots with the back foot raised completely off the ground.

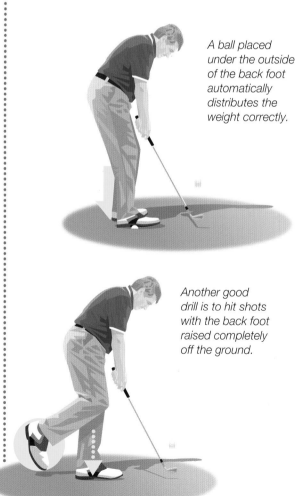

A ball placed under the outside of the back foot automatically distributes the weight correctly.

Another good drill is to hit shots with the back foot raised completely off the ground.

4.2

Let the **club** do the **work**

Most chipping problems occur because players try to help the ball into the air and onto the putting surface, rather than allowing the club and its natural loft to do the job for them. Just pick the spot where you want to land the ball and concentrate on making clean contact with it.

Q5

Your ball is sitting in fluffy light sand in a greenside trap and an explosion shot with your sand wedge is needed to get it onto the green. You estimate that the leading edge of the club needs to enter the sand 2 inches behind the ball. You should focus:

A Two inches **ahead** of the ball to ensure that you complete your swing.

B On the **back** edge of the ball.

C On **the spot** where you intend the club to enter the sand.

Q6

After carefully examining the contours of the green, you estimate and are fairly certain that there is about a 6-inch break from right to left on the 15-foot putt you have to play. You:

A Stand with your feet, hips, and shoulders **all left** of the hole and use a slice spin to counteract the break.

B Pick a spot to **the right** of the hole and play a straight putt to it.

C Bang it **hard** at the hole to eliminate the effect of the break.

Q7 Standing behind the ball and in a direct line with the hole, you decide to try the plumb–bobbing technique you have seen the professionals using in televised tournaments. Closing one eye and holding the club so that the shaft bisects the ball, the pin appears on the right of the shaft. The putt will:

A Break to **the right.**

 Break to **the left.**

Q8 Your ball has come to rest on the fairway several yards from the green and your partner suggests that your best option is to play the "Texas Wedge." This entails using:

A The **putter** to run the ball onto the green.

B The **special wedge** created to nip the ball off tight fairway lies, such as those found on many Texas courses.

C The run-up shot played with **a fairway wood**, using a putting grip and action.

A good practice drill is to draw a line in the sand where you want the club to enter.

Answer: **B**

All putts should be played as straight ones, so the correct way to play putts affected by the contours and breaks of a green is to pick the spot where you estimate you have to putt to and line up squarely with it. Let the break then take the ball to the hole. Banging the ball at the hole hard enough to eliminate the effect of the break should be attempted from only a few feet.

Aim for this spot

Answer: **C**

A5

Looking at the exact spot where you want the leading edge of the clubhead to enter the sand will help achieve your objective. A good practice drill is to draw a line in the sand behind the ball and where you want the club to enter. By playing the shot, you can see exactly where contact with the sand is made. Remember that this can be carried out only during practice.

Pick a spot where you estimate you have to putt to, and line up squarely with it.

When plumb-bobbing, make sure that the bottom of the shaft appears to pass through the center of the ball.

A8 Answer: A

The "Texas Wedge" shot is when the ball is hit with a putter along the ground and onto the green. It is a useful shot to have in your repertoire when a high wind threatens to blow the ball off line, even from only a few yards off the green, and this shot is often used on links courses. The grass between ball and green must, of course, be fairly short and the ground free from bumps to throw the ball off line.

A7 Answer: A

Plumb-bobbing is used by some top players to ascertain how a putt will break. Stand or squat on even ground behind the ball in line with the hole and hold the putter loosely at the bottom of the grip so that it hangs vertically. Close one eye and position the club so that the bottom of the shaft appears to pass through the center of the ball. Holding the putter steady, look up the shaft to see on which side the flagstick appears. Whichever side it appears on is the direction to which the ball will break. The further it appears off center, the greater the break.

The "Texas wedge" is particularly useful on windy days.

Soft hands
for success

4.3

Most poor short-game players make the common mistake of gripping their clubs too tightly. This normally results in the clubface closing (to produce erratic shots) and tension spreading to the arms and shoulders. Remember—delicate shots around the green call for soft hands.

Q9 A particular golden rule is quoted by virtually all the leading teachers and touring professionals when advising amateurs, especially high-handicappers, on how to play chip shots from just off the green. You should:

A Get the ball **rolling** on the green as soon as you can.

B Take away uncertainty by **flighting** the ball all the way to the pin.

C Play the shot with plenty of **backspin** so you can get it to check close to the hole on its second or third bounce.

Q10 Your ball has come to rest on an awkward little downslope in a greenside trap. You remember that to give yourself a reasonable chance of success your body should be angled to reflect the slope, but you are confused about where the ball should be positioned in your address. It should be:

A Between the center of your stance and the inside of the **front foot.**

B Between the center of your stance and the inside of the **back foot.**

C In the **center** of the feet.

Q11 An acceptable variation of the reverse overlap putting grip entails running the outstretched forefinger of the lower hand down the shaft of the club. Which group of players particularly benefit from this type of grip?

A Those who **flick at the ball** rather than stroke all the way through it.

B Those whose **top hand** is naturally dominant.

C Those whose **lower hand** is naturally dominant.

Q12 The use of the lofted wood to chip the ball when it is close to the green has been made popular during recent seasons by top tournament stars. What type of lie is generally regarded suitable for this somewhat unorthodox but very effective method of getting the ball near the pin?

A Sitting **on the top** of semirough.

B Sitting **down in** semirough.

C Very little or **no grass** under the ball.

Remember to examine the green for any contours and breaks to establish the spot to where you should chip, and to predict the path of the ball once it starts rolling.

A10 Answer: B

The correct position for the ball when playing from a downslope is between the center of your stance and the inside of the back foot. Any further forward and you risk digging the club into the sand well before the ball and leaving it in the trap. Remember also that a wider-than-normal stance is needed to set your body at 90 degrees to the slope and about 80 percent of your body weight needs to be concentrated on the front foot. The shot is played with a sharp wrist break, keeping the weight on the front foot so you feel you are swinging down the slope rather than trying to scoop the ball out.

You should feel as though you are swinging down the slope when faced with this tricky shot.

 # Answer: A

The golden rule is to get the ball rolling on the putting surface as soon as you possibly can—simply because it is much easier to judge a roll than an unpredictable bounce when the ball is flighted at the hole. As far as club selection is concerned, choose one with just enough loft to clear the longer grass and get the ball onto the green.

Answer: C

Placing the forefinger of the lower hand down the shaft of the putter is a good alternative to the orthodox reverse overlap grip for players who tend to generate more feel with the lower hand and favor pushing the clubhead through the ball rather than pulling it through impact with their higher hand.

The fairway wood makes an excellent "chipper" when the ball is sitting on a bare lie.

Placing the forefinger of the lower hand down the shaft of the putter also helps to ensure that the hands remain square to the target through the impact area.

Answer: C

Using a fairway wood to chip the ball onto the green is particularly successful when it is sitting down a little in grass or has come to rest on a bare or sandy lie. Tiger Woods regularly uses this shot and proves what excellent results can be achieved by gripping down the club and using a normal putting stance and action to strike the ball in its center and allow topspin to take it to the hole—and often into it.

4.4

Anything goes in **putting**

Putting is probably the most frustrating part of the game. Although certain basic fundamentals apply, virtually any method that works is okay to use. Don't be afraid to experiment with various types of putters, your grip, set-up, and stroke—however off-beat they may seem.

Q13

The position of the ball in relation to the eyes is considered of paramount importance when it comes to putting. What is considered to be the ideal position to promote the desired pendulum action and to correctly determine the line of the putt?

A Directly **below** the eyes.

B **Outside** the line of the eyes.

C Just **inside** the line of the eyes.

Q14

When faced with an uphill chip to a flag on a green sloping upward from front to back, many players are not sure how it should be played and usually pay the price of indecision by leaving the ball well short. The shot is best played with:

A A lob or **sand wedge.**

B A **pitching wedge.**

C A **less lofted iron** (such as a 6, 7, or 8).

Q15 Your ball has come to rest in a greenside trap. Although it is sitting nicely on an even lie, the pin is positioned just behind the 5-foot lip of the trap, demanding a shot that will stop fairly quickly when it lands on the putting surface. You have read that your feet, hips, and shoulders should be aimed to the left of the target, but the leading edge of the clubface should be set:

Q16 On landing, a chip shot played from the rough around the green usually reacts differently from one played from cut grass and a normal lie. If you are faced with such a shot, you would expect the ball to:

A Possess plenty of **backspin** and stop immediately upon landing.

A **Straight** at the pin.

B Slightly **open** (pointing right of the pin).

B **Bounce forward** on landing but then pull up sharply on the second (possibly third) bounce.

C Slightly **closed** (pointing left of the pin).

C **Roll more** on landing than if played from cut grass.

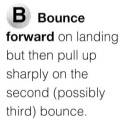

Drop a ball from the bridge of your nose to find the right spot.

Answer: C

Most high-handicappers are guilty of leaving the ball well short when faced with a chip to a green that slopes from front to back. And it is usually as a result of playing the shot with a club with too much loft on its face. Lob, sand, and pitching wedges are not the clubs to reach for, because their lofted faces all create far too much spin and cause the ball to pull up quickly on landing, rather than run to the hole. Best results are obtained with the 6, 7, or 8 iron. All hit the ball lower with less spin and allow it to release up the slope with plenty of roll. Experiment to establish which of the clubs give you the best results and save pars around the green.

A13

Answer: A

The best place for your eyes is directly over the ball. If they are inside the line you will almost certainly push your putt to the right and having them outside the line nearly always results in a pull to the left. An easy and effective way to find the correct position is to take up your normal putting stance with your face parallel to the ground and drop a ball from the bridge of your nose. Where it lands is the perfect spot for it to be positioned at address.

Experiment to discover which clubs will give you the best results.

The best way to ensure success is to open the face and adopt your grip before stepping into the trap. Lining your feet, hips, and shoulders to the left of the target will automatically put the clubface in the correct position for the shot.

A16   Answer: C

Hitting the ball from the rough nearly always results in grass becoming trapped between the clubface and the ball, preventing the grooves from doing their job—namely, putting backspin on the ball. As a result, the ball will roll further than normal when it lands on the green.

If your ball happens to be in long grass quite near the green, the best way of playing is to position it further back than normal in your stance to enable the clubface to make as clean a contact as possible.

A15   Answer: B

Holding the clubface slightly open (pointing right of the pin) will allow you to swing along the line of your feet, hips, and shoulders and automatically cut nicely under the ball, sending it high out of the sand and causing it to stop fairly quickly on the green. Many high–handicappers make the mistake of trying to manipulate the clubface open after they have taken up their stance in the sand. This very often fails to work, as the hands usually return to their natural position and the clubface squares, causing the ball to fly lower than desired.

Expect the ball to roll more on landing when playing from long grass.

In Trouble

5

No golfer likes to hit his or her ball into trouble. But the stark fact is that, even if you are a top professional tour player, it's an inevitable part of any round of golf. Anyway, just think how boring the game would be without hazards! Few situations occur on the course where you have no choice other than to declare your ball totally unplayable. Study this section carefully and you will learn how to turn potential disaster into delight. Even playing the ball from shallow water can become part of your repertoire of Houdini-like escape acts.

5.1

Rise to the challenge

Players who regard the rough and bunkers as challenges are usually the ones who cope best when their ball lands and finishes off the fairway. Those who curse their luck are nearly always the ones who perform badly in such situations.

Q1 Your tee shot lands in deep and heavy rough about 200 yards from the hole, making it impossible for you to reach the green with your next shot. Your main objective, therefore, is to take a very lofted club and get the ball out of the long grass and onto the fairway by the most direct route. Where should the ball be positioned to give you the best chance of getting it in the air and back onto the short grass?

A Just **inside** the left heel.

B In the **center** of your stance.

C Between center and the **back foot**.

Q2 Your ball has come to rest about 10 yards behind a tree and 130 yards from the front of the green. It is sitting quite well in light rough and you have a direct route to the flag if you can play it under one of the outstretched branches. Intending to play a punch shot with a mid iron, you:

A Ensure that you achieve your **usual** follow-through after impact.

B Concentrate on making a **higher-than-normal** finishing position.

C Restrict the follow-through to **less than normal**.

Q3 Talk about bad luck. Not only has your ball gone into a greenside trap, but three-quarters of it is buried in the sand. You remember that you have to stand square to the target line and set the leading edge of your sand wedge squarely behind the ball, but you are not entirely certain how the shot is played. You should:

A Break your wrists almost as soon as you **start** your takeaway.

B Make a nice **smooth** takeaway with little wrist break.

C Use no wrist break at all and use your upper-body strength to **power** the ball out.

 Q4 Despite the laughs from your playing partners, you decide to have a go at playing your ball from the shallow water in the edge of a lake adjoining the fairway. Having taken off your socks and shoes and rolled up your trousers, you grip your sand wedge and prepare to play the ball. As far as hitting it is concerned, you should aim:

A At the **top** of the ball.

B A couple of inches **behind** the ball.

C A couple of inches **ahead** of the ball.

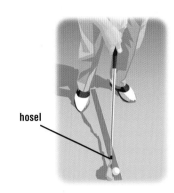

Positioning the ball in the back of your stance will help ensure it escapes from the long grass.

hosel

A2 **Answer: C**

Having set the ball back in the stance and pushing your hands ahead of it, your main swing thoughts should be to make a compact backswing and keep your body weight over the ball as you go through the impact zone. These actions will result in a low and restricted follow–through, with your arms finishing roughly parallel with the ground. Remember to give careful consideration to club selection when faced with this situation. Success very much depends on using a club with enough loft to get the ball airborne from the light rough but on a low enough trajectory to prevent it hitting the branch.

A1 **Answer: C**

The object of the exercise is to prevent the long and thick grass from grabbing the hosel and clubhead, which would rob the club of its speed, clubface squareness, and loft. Positioning the ball between the center of your stance and the back foot will result in a backswing with plenty of wrist break to obtain the required steep angle of attack into the ball and contact before the long and thick grass takes its toll. Many high-handicappers and novices position the ball inside the left heel when they are faced with this shot, because they think it will give them extra loft. That, unfortunately, is one of the reasons why they remain high-handicappers!

If you play the punch shot correctly, your arms should finish roughly parallel with the ground.

Answer: A

A shallow angle of attack into the partly buried ball will result in the clubhead coming into contact with too much sand and the loss of sufficient power and speed to get it airborne. It is vital, therefore, to create an upright swing and a steep descent into the ball. This is achieved by positioning the ball back in the stance and then breaking your wrists as soon as the backswing is started. A full backswing should also be used so that sufficient speed can be generated in the downswing to force the clubhead through the sand and remove the ball.

Breaking your wrists early will create the required steep angle of attack into the ball.

Answer: B

To enable the club to get down and under the ball, you need to hit at least two inches behind where you see it. Water has a magnifying effect and creates the impression that the ball is nearer the surface than it actually is, so you must examine the situation very carefully. Having decided to play, hover the club above the spot where it must enter the water, and then pick it up steeply in the backswing to obtain the necessary angle of attack into the ball. Hit down firmly to combat the resistance of the water, to about the same degree as playing from a ball buried in a sand trap. This shot should never be attempted by amateurs if the ball is lying more than an inch below the surface.

Aim two inches behind the ball when it is in shallow water and it will splash out—literally!

5.2

Prepare for those **problems**

Many players fail to cope with trouble shots simply because they never practice them. Why not spend your next practice session playing balls from deep grass, plugged lies in the sand, and divots? You will then be fully prepared to deal with in-play problems.

Q5

Your ball has come to rest in a greenside sand trap and you have no chance at all of playing it within the trap itself. The shot demands that you stand on the lip of the trap and well above the ball. Your stance and spine angle will naturally dictate a fairly upright and steep swing path, and you must be careful that you do not topple over backward before you hit the ball. You should:

A Stab the ball out with no follow-through.

B Restrict the follow-through to about **half** that of normal.

C Go for a **full** follow-through.

Q6

Although you have hit a good second shot to a par 5 hole, it has come up short and a few yards to the side of the green on a steep and tricky little down slope. When you take your address position, you should play the ball:

A In the **center** of your stance.

B Between center and the **front** foot.

C Between center and the **back** foot.

Q7 It's proving to be just one of those days! At long last you have connected perfectly with your driver and the ball has gone like a rocket 250 yards straight down the middle of the fairway…only to come to rest in a divot. After mumbling some choice words about the player who removed the chunk of fairway, you calm down and prepare to play. To achieve success, you position your hands at address:

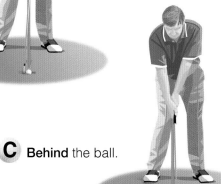

A **Ahead** of the ball.

B **Level** with the ball.

C **Behind** the ball.

Q8 It's the final hole of a match play competition, you are all even, and your ball has landed on cut grass but with a tree blocking a direct path to the green. Your opponent's second shot has put him on the green and, in order to keep yourself in contention, you have no alternative other than to play an intentional hook. To help achieve the desired right-to-left flight path, you must adopt a tophand grip:

A With **less** than two knuckles showing.

B With **two knuckles** showing.

C With **more** than two knuckles showing.

Thoughts of a full follow-through will help ensure success when faced with this shot.

A6 Answer: C

When faced with a shot from a down slope, many high-handicappers make the big mistake of thinking that the ball should be played forward of center in order to achieve loft. In fact, it has to be played back in the stance to prevent the clubhead from striking the ground before impact. The slope will, of course, have the effect of robbing the clubface of some of its loft. But this problem is solved by simply selecting a club with more loft than is usually required for the distance to be covered. As far as setup is concerned, one way of getting it right is to remember to allow your body to reflect the shape of the slope. So, weight should be concentrated more on the front foot when playing on a down slope.

Don't make the common mistake of playing the ball forward in the stance.

A5 Answer: C

To stand any chance of success with this shot, you must try to keep everything as smooth as possible, otherwise you will finish flat on your back in the sand. Although, because of your setup, it will not be possible to make a full follow-through, thinking about one and trying to attain one will help create sufficient energy and smoothness to get the ball out of the sand. Thoughts of a stab shot or restricting the backswing will lead to a jerky action, and almost certainly another sand trap shot!

Answer: A

Playing from a divot demands a steep angle of attack into the ball, so you adopt a stance where the ball is opposite the heel of your back foot and the hands level with the front thigh. Although the shot itself is not particularly difficult, it is important to remember that the ball is sure to fly out on a lower-than-normal trajectory; so select a club with a little more loft (say a 7 instead of a 6) than you would normally use for the distance you are seeking. A good thought to have while playing this shot is to try to drive the ball even further into the ground at impact. It will help prevent you from making the disastrous mistake of trying to scoop it up and causing a thin contact.

Try to drive the ball further into the ground, rather than scooping it from the divot.

Answer: C

In addition to aiming the feet, hips, and shoulders a little right of target, a strong grip combines to promote an intentional hook, where the ball sets off right of target and draws back to the line—one of the shots needed to negotiate the ball around obstacles such as trees. A neutral grip is generally regarded as one where you can see two or two-and-a-half knuckles of the top hand when you look down on it at address. To help promote a hook, the two hands move around the grip until the third knuckle of the top hand appears in view.

Flight path of ball

Moving the hands so that at least three knuckles can be seen on the top hand helps to achieve an intentional hook shot.

5.3

Learn to take your medicine

If your ball lands in deep trouble, concentrate on getting it back into a playable position, rather than chasing rainbows and attempting something only achievable with a lifetime's best shot. The road to high scores is paved with impossible shots.

Q9 A poor tee shot has resulted in the ball coming to rest in the rough and about 180 yards from the front of the green. It is not sitting too far down in the grass and, because of the state of your match play game, you decide you will have a go at getting it onto the putting surface. Which club will give you the best chance of success?

A A long or mid iron.

B A fairway wood.

Q10 Your ball has skipped through the green and come to rest on a hard patch of dry, bare earth under some tall trees. You need to play the shot with a little loft to clear a few unpredictable humps and bumps and land the ball on the green. Which club/clubs do you use for the shot?

A A sand wedge.   **B** A pitching wedge.

C A 9 iron.

Q11 A sliced tee shot means that your only path into the green is over the top of a group of trees. You work out that, in order to gain extra height, the ball needs to be further forward than normal in the stance. What else can you do to help achieve the shot pattern you require?

A Stand a **little farther** than normal away from the ball at address.

B Stand a **little closer** than normal to the ball at address.

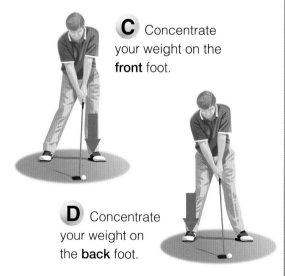

C Concentrate your weight on the **front** foot.

D Concentrate your weight on the **back** foot.

Q12 You are facing one of the trickiest shots in the game. Your approach chip has run by the pin and you are now looking at a very sharp downhill putt, with a sand trap waiting at the bottom of the slope, if you charge the ball too far beyond the cup. Which of the following is a recognized way of helping to make sure the ball is not struck too hard?

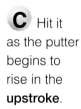

A Hit it off the **toe** of the putter.

B Hit it off the **heel** of the putter.

C Hit it as the putter begins to rise in the **upstroke**.

D Hit it on the **downstroke**.

Lofted fairway woods are ideal for removing the ball from rough that is not too severe.

 Answer: B

The design of the sole of fairway woods make them a better choice for the club golfer trying to achieve both escape and distance from the rough. Long grass tends to grab at the hosel of irons, forcing them to twist and lose their effective loft. For this reason, trying to hit a long or mid iron to a green about 180 yards away is beyond the capabilities of most club players. The rounded and smooth soles of fairway woods glide through long grass much easier, making them ideal for this particular shot.

 **Answer: B C**

The sand wedge has bounce built into the sole to stop it from digging too deeply into the sand—as a result of this, the leading edge is raised a little off the ground at address. This design would cause the club to bounce off the hard ground and skid into the middle of the ball, causing a thinned and uncontrollable contact. Most pitching wedges, on the other hand, are designed without too much bounce, and their leading edges are able to get to the bottom of the ball and pick it off hard ground. If you have any doubt about whether your pitching wedge has too much bounce for this particular shot, reach for the 9 iron.

Don't make the mistake of reaching for the sand wedge when playing from a bare lie.

Answer: B

Standing a little closer than normal to the ball at address, coupled with a more upright posture, results in an upright swing to generate extra loft. Also concentrate on keeping your head behind the ball a little longer than normal through the impact zone and then going on to achieve a high finishing position. One word of warning with this shot: make sure that placing the ball forward in the stance doesn't pull your shoulders into an open position at address.

Hitting the ball off the toe of the putter will produce a slower roll.

Answer: A

You are faced with a tricky downhill putt and the prospect of running into a sand trap if you charge the ball past the hole. The best solution is to strike it with your normal strength for this particular length of putt, but, off the toe of the putter, rather than the center. This will result in less energy being produced and the ball leaving the face at a slower speed. Any alteration to your normal putting technique on this shot will probably result in the very last thing you are seeking—a jerky action lacking control, and deceleration of the clubhead at impact.

Stand closer to the ball and adopt an upright posture for a high-flying shot.

The Elements

6

Now and then, whether we like it or not, we find ourselves out on the course having to play in conditions we wouldn't wish on our worst enemies. A good knowledge of how to adapt your game successfully when the going gets tough is often the difference between wringing a winning score from the 18 holes, or cursing your luck and clutching for excuses for a dismal performance. The questions in this section will help you determine whether you are an all-weather wonder or a real damp squib.

Playing Against the Elements

6.1

Don't adopt an **attitude problem**

Poor players will normally curse bad weather conditions—which is why they usually perform worse when the going gets tough. Good players, on the other hand, treat it as a challenge and enjoy adapting their games to suit the day.

Q1 You have reached a 175-yard par 3 hole and there's a fairly stiff wind blowing into your face. Having selected the club you think is correct to cover the required distance—a 3 iron—you:

A Adopt your **normal** stance.

B Stand with your feet **closer together** than normal.

C Stand with your feet **wider apart** than normal.

Q2 It's raining very heavily and you notice that your opponent has reached for a 6 iron rather than his normal 7 iron to play a shot of 145 yards from the fairway to the green. What is the probable reason for his decision?

A To help keep a **better balance**.

B Rain on the clubface increases **backspin** on the ball, so your opponent needs an extra club to compensate.

C Water in the dimples of the ball will cause it to **lose distance** through the air.

Q3 You notice on an icy cold and wet day that after playing each hole your opponent pops the ball into one of his pockets and from another pocket produces another ball (of exactly the same make, specification, and number) with which to play the next hole. What is the probable thinking behind his actions?

A To keep the ball **warm**.

B To avoid having to **clean and dry** the ball every time he faces a tee shot.

C To cause **even wear** on both balls so that their playing characteristics will be exactly the same in the event of one of them being lost.

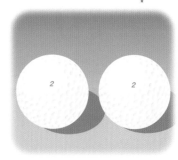

Q4 The sand in a greenside trap has become saturated and clogged by heavy rain and you need to get the ball over the front lip and onto the green. Your caddy hands you the pitching wedge rather than the sand wedge so that the bounce built into the latter club will not cause the leading edge to skid into the center of the ball. What must you now do to give yourself a reasonable chance of success?

A Open the clubface at address.

B Close the clubface at address.

C Square the clubface at address.

The width of your feet should be wider than normal at address when playing into the wind.

Wind direction

Answer: A

Wet weather play presents several problems, including loss of grip by the hands on the club and by the feet on the ground. An excellent strategy to help solve the latter when conditions are slippery underfoot is to take at least one club stronger than you would normally use for the distance and swing with no more than 80 percent of your usual effort. Also remember to check before play that the spikes in your shoes are in good condition and that, during play, they do not become clogged by grass and mud.

Swinging well within yourself will help maintain good balance when conditions underfoot are slippery.

Answer: C

It is extremely important when facing a shot into a stiff wind to establish a solid base so that balance can be retained throughout. Widening the stance by standing with your feet a little farther apart than normal (about 3 to 4 inches for someone of average height and build) helps to achieve this. Another benefit from adopting a slightly wider stance is that it automatically shortens the swing and keeps the overall movement more compact. Warning: do not make the mistake of widening your stance too much, which will restrict the required amount of body turn needed to make a successful swing.

Swing no more than 80 percent of your full power

Answer: A

It is a fact that the spin rate of golf balls, particularly those of wound construction, and the distances they travel are affected by temperature. Tests have revealed that the carry (or fly) distance of a wound balata ball is reduced by about 10 yards on a cold day compared with a warm one. Keeping a couple of golf balls warm in your pocket on a cold day and playing each of them on alternate holes therefore translates into extra yardage on your shots.

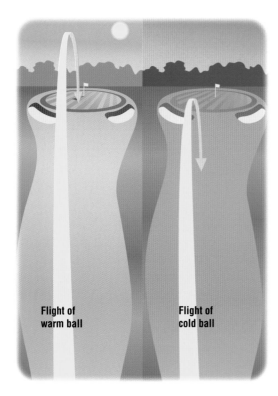

Flight of warm ball   **Flight of cold ball**

The flight of a warm ball will be about 10 yards or meters further than that of a cold ball.

Answer: C

Greenside shots from sand traps call for a different style of play when the sand becomes saturated and clogged by heavy rain. Instead of opening the face of a sand wedge and splashing the ball out on a cushion of sand, you need to counteract the greater resistance of the wet and clogged grains by keeping the clubface of a pitching wedge square and striking the sand much closer to the ball than you normally would in dry conditions. Don't make the common mistake of trying to help the ball into the air with a scooping action.

Hit under and through the ball with a square clubface.

Playing Against the Elements

6.2

A chance to **experiment**

Don't expect to score as well when the weather conditions are bad. If you are playing a non-competitive round, use it as an opportunity to experiment with those shots that have recently been causing you problems.

Q6

It's been raining very heavily for the past hour and your ball is lying about 10 yards from the green. The grass between the ball and the putting surface is a little on the long side. Knowing you have to clear the longer grass and land the ball on the green, you remove a lofted club from your bag. You expect the ball to:

Q5

You are on a high tee and there's a strong wind blowing across the long par 4 hole from right to left. Trailing in the match and knowing you need reasonable distance to make sure you hit the green with your second shot, you should:

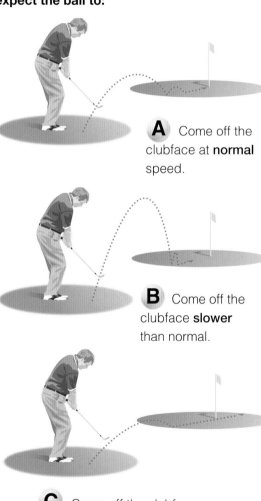

A Come off the clubface at **normal** speed.

B Come off the clubface **slower** than normal.

C Come off the clubface **faster** than normal.

Wind direction

A Aim to the **right** of the fairway, allowing for the wind to bring it back on target.

Wind direction

B Aim **left** and play a fade to make sure as far as you can that the ball stays on the cut grass.

Wind direction

C Aim at the **center** of the fairway and tee the ball very low with the intention of keeping it straight and under the wind.

Q7 You arrive at your club and, although it's not raining, the course is wet and soggy as a result of an overnight downpour, and the club officials have ruled that bags have to be carried. You decide to lighten your load by reducing the number of clubs you have to carry. Which are best left in the car?

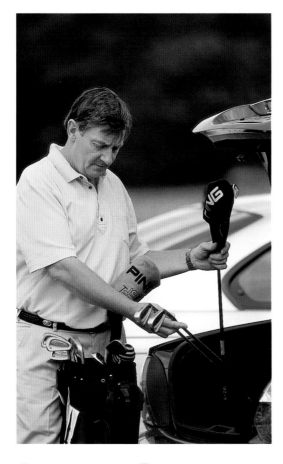

A Long **irons.**   **B** Fairway **woods.**

Q8 A stiff wind is blowing from right to left, and you are facing a shot at a 160-yard par 3 hole into a fairly small green. Deciding that your only realistic chance of keeping the ball on the green is to fade the ball in, you reach for a club. You select:

A Your **normal** club for the distance.

B One with **more loft** than normal.

C One with **less loft** than normal.

Let the wind be your friend whenever you can.

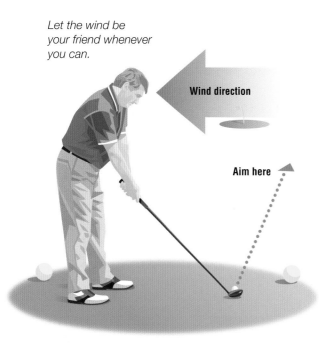

Wind direction

Aim here

Answer: C

You can expect water to build up on the clubface when you play this shot, and that means the grip between the club and the ball at impact will be reduced, generally resulting in less backspin. So expect the ball to fly off the face faster than normal and to run farther on landing (although the latter could be offset in this instance by the wet grass on the putting surface). Remember always to take full advantage when preferred lies apply. Cleaning your ball and wiping the clubface before playing the shot will help eliminate unpredictability.

Answer: A

When seeking distance from the tee, if the wind is blowing across the hole, use it to help your cause rather than battle against it. In this case, aim to the right and let the wind blow the ball back and onto the fairway. It will land with the wind behind, causing it to roll farther than normal. Don't make the mistake of trying to fade the ball into the fairway. All this will do is hold it up against the wind, robbing you of the distance you need through the air and inducing a lack of roll on landing. Teeing the ball low invariably produces a steep angle of attack, leading to the clubhead chopping under the ball and a high trajectory shot. In this instance, the ball would finish short and in trouble on the left.

Clean your ball whenever you get the chance, if the rules of the day allow it.

Because of their overall design and size, lofted woods' sweet spots are larger than those of long irons.

 Answer: A

Most amateurs find long irons hard to hit at the best of times, and they become even more unforgiving in wet and soggy conditions. Unless hit perfectly, the leading edges of their faces can easily make contact with the ground before the ball, resulting in loss of both distance and accuracy. Lofted woods are easier to use because the soles of their clubheads slide more easily through wet grass. Their centers of gravity are also much lower, making it easier to get the ball airborne.

A8 **Answer: C**

Any shot played with fade or slice spin will result in less distance. In this instance, you would therefore select a stronger club than usual for the required yardage. As far as actually playing the shot is concerned, the most simple method is to adopt your normal grip on the club and stand with your shoulders, hips, and feet aiming left of target and with the face of the club open and pointing toward the pin. Swinging along the line of your feet and the open clubface will combine to impart the fade spin required.

Remember to select a club with less loft than you would normally use when playing an intentional fade.

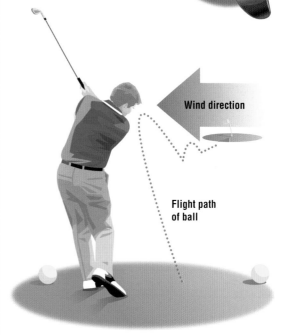

Wind direction

Flight path of ball

Tactics

7

No matter how good a technique you have developed and how well you strike the ball, low scores and match play victories are virtually impossible to achieve if your course management skills and tactics are neglected. A few seconds spent on each tee planning exactly how you intend to play the hole ahead is often the sole difference between a highly satisfying and enjoyable game and a nightmarish round. This section is designed to reveal whether you are a good thinker or one of those hapless souls who spends his or her golfing career lost in a sea of high scores.

Tactics

7.1 Where the games are won

Don't make the game's biggest tactical error of trying to match the efforts of a long-hitting opponent. Although long drives are great to hit and watch, the outcome of a game usually depends on the accuracy of approach shots onto the greens and your putting skills.

Q1 You have reached the finals of your club's match play championship and your opponent is a real tiger—he plays a handicap of 2 compared with your 18. The first hole is a long par 4, lined by trees on the right. You have won the toss of the coin and are due to play the first shot of the match. A good idea would be to:

A Take your driver and dent your opponent's confidence by trying to hit a long shot and prove to him that he has a **tough match** on his hands.

B Take the **safe option** and elect to play a lofted wood or iron to save you the embarrassment of a botched drive.

Q2 You have to play your second shot into a green with a large horseshoe-shaped bunch of trees behind. You have never played the venue before and, although there are no yardage indicators on the course, it looks like you are 150 yards from the center of the green. You should select:

A Your **normal** club for the distance.

B One club **stronger** than normal.

C One club **weaker** than normal.

Q3 There are tall pines all along the left side of the par 4 hole you are about to play and you decide that the best chance of success is to fade the ball away from them by using your driver. As far as teeing the ball is concerned, what is the best thing to do to help promote the shape of shot you are seeking?

A Tee it at normal height.

B Tee it **higher** than normal.

C Tee it **lower** than normal.

Q4 This hole has a lake running along the entire length of the left side. From where would you advise a mid- or high-handicapper to tee the ball?

A The **left side** of the teeing ground.

B The **center** of the teeing ground.

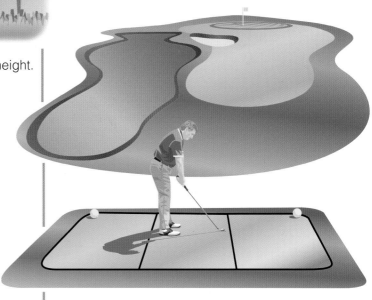

C The **right side** of the teeing ground.

Try not to make a mess of things at the start of the round.

 Answer: B

Trees or large objects behind a green often cause an optical illusion, giving the impression that the pin is nearer than it is. If you have no reliable information on the yardage, the best bet is to take one club stronger than your eyes tell you is needed. Exactly the reverse applies on holes where there is nothing visible behind the green. On these, the pins generally appear to be farther away than they are.

Take at least one extra club to allow for the optical illusion.

 Answer: B

It is important to get off to a strong start and put your opponent under pressure from the word go. The last thing you want to do is to make a complete mess of the first hole and present it to him as a gift, boosting his confidence and damaging your own. The wise decision here is to take the safer lofted wood or iron and give yourself a much better chance of hitting the fairway. If you get a shot, you should, at the least, be able to make a net par. Remember also that your opponent—no matter how good a player—is probably feeling just as nervous on the first tee as you are.

Answer: A

Mid- and high-handicappers are often worried when they are faced with shots where water can come into play. By teeing the ball on the left of the teeing area they can hit away from the trouble and need to concentrate only on hitting the fairway. The worst place to tee the ball for these players is on the right, where they will be looking straight at the watery grave.

A3 # Answer: C

Teeing the ball low with a driver normally encourages an out-to-in swing path into the ball and fade spin, causing the ball to travel from left to right and, in this case, away from the troublesome trees on the left. The amount of spin can also be dictated by weakening the grip (moving the hands a little to the left on the club) and aiming the feet, hips, and shoulders left of the target. The clubface should be set square at address.

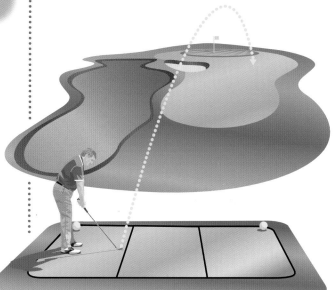

Help eliminate trouble by positioning yourself correctly on the teeing ground.

How high you tee the ball can affect the amount of side spin.

Tactics

7.2 Prepare for the **battle ahead**

Pre-round preparation and planning can sometimes prove almost as valuable as your armory of shots. If you are playing a particular venue for the first time, it's a good idea to pop into the pro's shop and ask for any tips on how to tackle the task ahead.

Q5 When it comes to the tough question of conceding short putts to opponents in match play events, what is generally regarded as the best strategy?

A Concede **all putts** less than 8 inches.

B Concede **nothing**.

C Concede **randomly**.

Q6 On a calm day and faced with a pitch shot of about 80 yards to a pin in the middle of a flat green, where should the average player aim to land the ball?

A On the **front** of the green.

B On the top of the **pin**.

C On the **back** of the green.

Q7 Your singles match play game is at a critical stage. You have reached the 17th tee and, as a result of a really bad approach shot with your wedge on the hole you have just played, your one-hole advantage has gone and the position is all even. The going has been very slow, and the foursome up ahead has only just started the hole, meaning you face a probable wait of a few minutes before you can tee off. You:

A Examine why you hit such a bad shot on the last hole and keep your mind fully **concentrated** on what lies ahead.

B Try to **relax** by chatting to your opponent or occupy your mind with something other than the game.

Q8 More water! You have to hit the ball over the lake to the flat green 150 yards away, and the pin is positioned 10 yards from the front. Knowing that you normally hit your 5 iron 160 yards, is it best to:

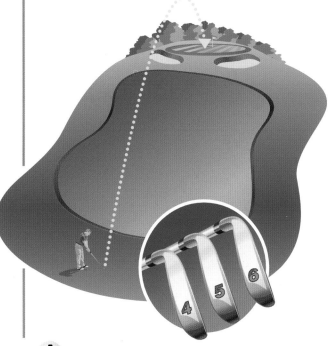

A Go ahead and use the **5 iron**?

B Take a **4 iron** and play within yourself?

C Use a **6 iron** and give it a really good whack to ensure you don't pull out of the shot?

Keep your opponent guessing.

 Answer: B C

All but the best amateur players make the big mistake of leaving their pitch shots well short of the pin, often putting themselves in three-putt territory. If you don't believe it, think how many times during a round of golf you actually hit the ball past the hole (tops and sculls not included!). One of the best ways of getting the ball near the pin and setting up a one-putt green is to aim to bring the ball down right on top of the pin or just beyond it. The chances are—based on the assumption that no one hits the ball as far as they think they are going to—that the ball will still finish short of the pin, but not three putts short.

 Answer: C

The best putting tactic in match play events is to keep your opponent guessing at all times. Conceding either all or no short putts of about 8 inches or less will make things much too predictable for them. By conceding some but asking for others to be holed does not allow them to get into a comfortable groove and often results in missed short putts when the pressure is on. Some players adopt a strategy of conceding all short putts early in the round and then asking for them to be holed as the game progresses and things begin to heat up.

There are no prizes for leaving the ball short when pitching.

Bouncing the ball up and down on your clubface will take your mind off the game until you want to turn up your concentration level.

A8 # Answer: B

Tension causes most players, particularly mid- and high-handicappers, to try to hit the ball much too hard when faced with a shot over water. The result is inevitably a wet ball. Knowing that you have more than enough club in your hands to cover the required distance will automatically slow down your swing and enable you to achieve the necessary smooth action.

A7 # Answer: B

Thinking about your recent mistake will do nothing to help your confidence for the battle ahead. And trying to concentrate for several hours at a time on the game is virtually impossible. The best thing to do is to chat with your playing partner or, if he's unwilling to do so, occupy your mind with something else until just before you are due to play your tee shot—then turn the concentration level to full power.

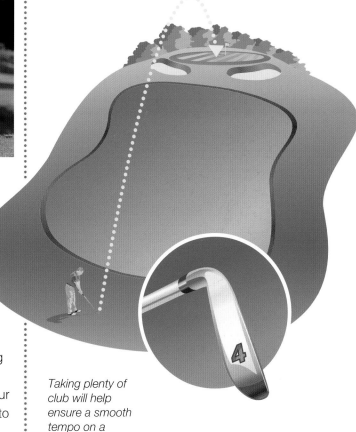

Taking plenty of club will help ensure a smooth tempo on a difficult shot.

7.3

Play your **natural shape**

If you are in a competitive situation and your natural shot is a fade, then play the course and your opponent with your normal game—don't attempt to change the pattern of your shots during the game. A driving range or practice ground is the place for such changes to be made.

Q9

What a hole! Wherever you look from the tee there's trouble—water all along the left, trees lining the right, and a gigantic bunker 160 yards directly in front. You stand on the right of the tee and look into the water, and standing on the left of the tee you see nothing but trees. In the middle you see both and, just to make matters worse, the sand trap as well. What can you do to remove the stress of aiming at trouble?

Q10

It's your honor and, thanks to using your shots wisely against your more experienced and low-handicap opponent, you are one up with two to play. The hole is a 160-yard par 3 and the pin is positioned on the left of the green directly behind a deep greenside trap. You should:

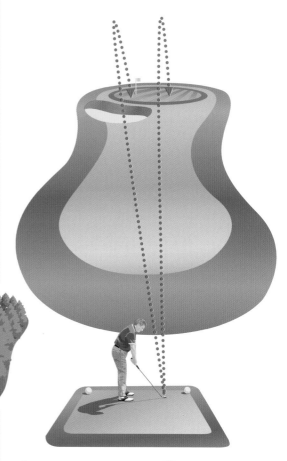

A Try to close out the game here and hit your ball at the flag, **risking** going into the trap.

B Play **conservatively** and go for the middle of the green, leaving the door open for your opponent to attack the hole.

Q11 A fairly stiff breeze is blowing into your face and you are left with an approach shot of 80 yards to the pin. Knowing that you normally hit your pitching wedge 100 yards, what is the best tactic to adopt?

Q12 You are facing your second shot into this par 5 hole, with the flag just over 300 yards away. It is beyond your capabilities to fly the ball over the water and reach the green, so what is the best strategy to adopt?

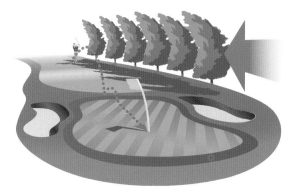

A Run the ball low with a **less lofted** club.

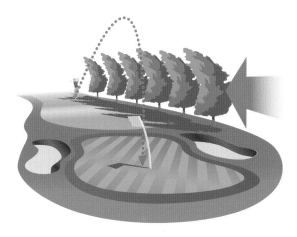

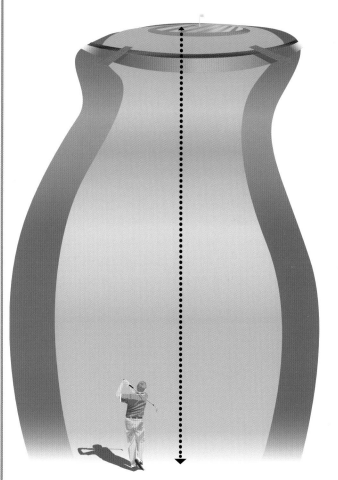

B Hit your **pitching wedge** flat out, knowing that the stiff breeze will restrict its distance to exactly what you require.

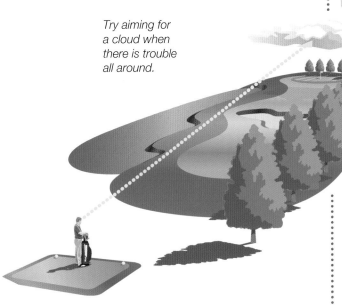

Try aiming for a cloud when there is trouble all around.

A10 Answer: B

You have spent 16 holes getting yourself into a match-winning position, so don't throw all your good work away. Hitting the easy part of the green will give you the strong possibility of a par and even an outside chance of a birdie. It will also give your opponent little option other than to take on a particularly difficult and perhaps match-losing shot. He will need nerves of steel to succeed. Putting your ball in the greenside trap will, on the other hand, almost certainly result in your experienced opponent playing for the middle of the green and winning the hole with a straightforward par. He will head to the last tee a confident man, whereas you will be thinking how you probably lost the match because of your lack of brain power on the last tee.

A9 Answer:

Most club golfers go to pieces when wood, sand, or water surrounds them on the tee. The usual result is that their anxiety causes them to come off the shot and the ball dives into the nearest trouble spot. The best way to combat the problem is to pick as your target an object on the skyline where you want the ball to travel. If there is nothing on the horizon, select a cloud. Mentally removing the trouble from your mind can work wonders. The ball should be sailing over that nasty cross bunker and heading toward the middle of the fairway when you look up after completing a nice smooth swing through impact!

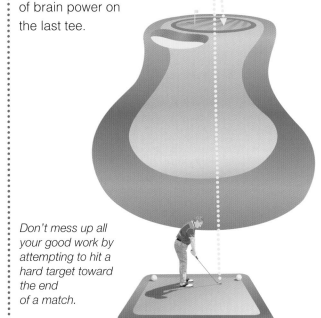

Don't mess up all your good work by attempting to hit a hard target toward the end of a match.

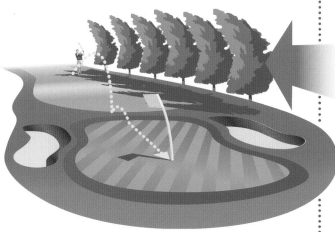

Try, whenever possible, to leave yourself a shot with your favorite club.

You have a much better chance of putting the ball near the pin if you play the ball under the wind.

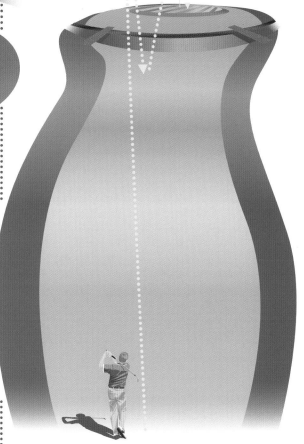

A11 Answer: A

Never hit a shot flat out, particularly wedges. Too fast a swing with a lofted club nearly always results in a shot pulled to the left of target because of too much independent involvement of the shoulders at the start of the downswing. The only sensible solution to the task ahead is to take a less lofted club, swing well within yourself, and run the ball under the stiff breeze and onto the green.

A12 Answer:

Hit the shot with a club that will leave you the next shot into the green with your favorite iron. There's nothing quite as good for the confidence as facing a shot over trouble with your best-performing club.

The Rules

8
Walk into any large and busy clubhouse, and you can be certain that one of the groups gathered at the bar or sitting at the tables will be talking about the rules. And it's no wonder, for no other sport is covered by as many rules regarding the playing of the game itself and the equipment used to play it. So, how well do *you* know the rules? In this chapter, we have taken a cross section of incidents that can happen during play and ask you to don the judge's robe.

The Rules

8.1

Laying down the **rules**

With the exception of the U.S. and Mexico (whose allegiances lie with the United States Golf Association) and Canada (which is self-governing), every other country has affiliated to the Royal and Ancient Golf Club. The following situations are applicable in both USGA and R&A countries.

Q1 A player searching for his ball discovers it has come to rest within a few inches of a bees' nest, with hundreds of angry bees swarming around. His match play opponent tells him that he has the choice of either playing the ball as it lies or conceding the hole and proceeding to the next tee. Is he correct?

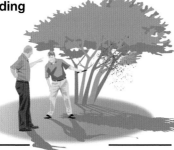

Q2 During a singles match play competition, the two players both hit their third shots into an area of thick rough and small shrubs. After unsuccessfully searching for the permitted five minutes they agree that, rather than go back and replay their shots, they will call the hole halved. Have they breached the rules?

Q3 You arrive at your ball in a match play event and find that it has come to rest just outside a sand trap, but you have no choice other than to stand inside it to play the shot. Without considering the rules, you automatically ground the club behind the ball and then touch the sand in the trap as you take the club back. Have you broken the rules? If so, what penalty, or penalties, have you incurred?

Q4 In the final round of the club's match play championship, Jim becomes increasingly angry at the fact that his opponent, Tom, continually looks into his bag while he (Jim) is playing each shot so he can determine what club is being used. He decides to prevent Tom from gaining information by covering the rest of his clubs with a towel. But, while Jim is playing his shot, Tom moves the towel to discover what he's using. "Peeping Tom" has infringed the rules by:

A Looking into the bag to seek information.

B Moving Jim's equipment (the towel) to find out what club he's using.

C Both A and B

Answer:

Avoid a potentially dangerous situation by dropping the ball nearby, but not nearer the hole.

No. The rules state it is not reasonable to expect anyone to have to play from this type of potentially dangerous situation or to suffer a penalty because he deems it unplayable. The player is therefore able to drop the ball on the nearest piece of "safe" ground as long as it is not nearer the hole. If the bees' nest and the ball happen to be in a hazard, the ball should, if possible, be dropped in the same hazard. If this is not possible, then it should be dropped in a nearby similar hazard or, with a one-stroke penalty, outside the hazard on the same line to the hole as the ball was lying, but not nearer the hole.

Answer:

No. Their agreement to declare the hole halved does not break the rules. The outcome would have been different, however, if they had agreed on the tee that, because the hole was a particularly difficult one, they would call it halved without either bothering to play a stroke. They would each then be disqualified from the competition.

In this situation, the players are allowed to declare the hole halved.

Answer:

A3 There has been no infringement of the rules. Because the ball itself wasn't actually lying in the sand, the normal rules relating to playing from within sand traps do not apply. The player was therefore perfectly entitled to ground the club behind the ball at address and make contact with any sand in the trap while playing this particular shot.

The player is entitled to make contact with the sand because the ball is just out of the trap.

Players are not allowed to gain information as a result of a physical act.

Answer: **B**

A4 Tom is perfectly at liberty to look into Jim's bag to discover what club he is playing into the green. Information obtained in this manner is not regarded as illegal advice. He did, however, fall foul of the rules when he moved the towel covering the rest of the clubs in the bag. Players are not permitted to gain information as a result of a physical act, so Tom automatically loses the hole. The penalty, if they had been playing in a stroke play competition, would have been two strokes.

8.2 Equipment can be **outlawed**

Manufacturers have to submit samples of proposed clubs and balls to the appropriate committees of their respective governing bodies for a ruling on whether their equipment conforms to the rules. Failure to do so runs the risk of the equipment being declared illegal for use in competitions.

Q5 A player finds that his ball has come to rest next to an out-of-bounds stake. Although his ball is lying in bounds, the stake itself interferes with his swing. Finding it is loose in the ground and can easily be removed, he pulls it out, plays his shot, and then puts it back in its hole. Is his action allowed within the rules?

Q6 Having hit his second shot from the fairway, a player thinks there is a chance that his ball has come to rest in a water hazard. Using one of the options open to him in Rule 26-1a, he hits another ball from the same spot. Walking up to the hazard he discovers that his original ball has, in fact, come to rest short of it and is lying in a playable position. What do the rules say?

Q7 A stroke play competition is halted when the committee suspends play because of lightning. Orders for play to resume are given, but one of the players—who previously had a lucky escape when lightning struck near him—claims that the danger has not passed and refuses to go back on the course. What do the rules say about this?

Q8 After holing out in an important stroke play competition, two players discover to their horror that they have holed out with each other's ball, although they have no doubt whatsoever that they were the balls they played from the teeing ground on that particular hole. The explanation could only have been that they had inadvertently exchanged balls during play of a previous hole or even between holes. Are they in breach of the rules and, if so, what penalties apply?

 Q9 A ball comes to rest where there is a sand trap in a direct line between it and the hole. The player walks into the trap to remove a rake that is directly on his line to the pin and to establish the lie of the land between the bunker and the green. On his way back he uses the rake to smooth out his footprints so that anyone who hits a ball into the trap will have a fair lie. Has he breached the rules?

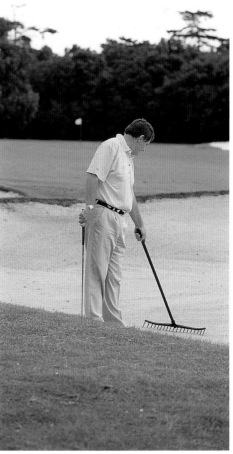

Moving anything on the course classed as fixed is a breach of the rules.

Answer:

A6

By not bothering to establish reasonably whether or not the original ball definitely went into the water hazard, this ball is deemed lost and the second ball is in play under penalty of stroke and distance.

Answer:

A7

The rules allow competitors to stop playing in a tournament if they believe that their safety is threatened by lightning. Committees are instructed not to risk exposing players to danger. If the committee considers that the danger has passed and that there is no further chance of lightning, they are entitled to order a resumption of play and disqualify any player who refuses to continue.

Answer:

A5

No, it is not permissible. Stakes marking out-of-bounds are classed as fixed, and moving anything on the course classed as such constitutes a breach of the rules. The penalty incurred in stroke play would be two shots, and in match play the loss of the hole. Incidentally, even if the player had realized his mistake and replaced the stake before playing his shot, he would still have been in breach of the rules and subject to the same penalties.

Players should not be put at risk by a ruling of the committee.

Answer:

Because it cannot be conclusively established that the exchange of balls occurred during the playing of a specific hole, the rules say the players should be given the benefit of the doubt. It is therefore assumed that the exchange of balls must have taken place between holes, and the players escape without penalty.

Mark your ball to avoid confusion.

If you wish to rake the sand in the bunker, do so after you have played your shot.

Answer:

Yes he has. A player who worsens his line to the hole is not entitled to restore it to its original condition. He would therefore lose the hole in a match play situation or two strokes if he was taking part in a stroke play event. To escape penalty and maintain etiquette, he should have played the shot and then gone into the trap to rake out the footprints he had made before restoring the rake to its original position.

The Rules

8.3

Buy your **own copy!**

A copy of the rules is usually available from your local golf club or any large bookstore. There are several excellent publications based on actual case histories and decisions on the rules, should you wish to explore the subject further.

Q10

Playing in a club medal competition and walking along the fairway toward the seventh green, Player A finds a ball that has been played by someone on an adjacent hole. This player (Player B) has by now declared it lost, elected to play another ball, and is walking toward his respective green. Player A calls to Player B that he has found the ball and Player B requests that it be returned. Because Player B is well beyond throwing distance, Player A takes an iron from his bag and hits it to him. A kind action by Player A, but has his kindness cost him a penalty?

Q11

A player hits a really long but very awkward wayward drive. Although it remains in bounds, it comes to rest behind a greenkeeping hut used to store course equipment, completely blocking the direct route to the green. The player optimistically says that by opening the door and one of the windows of the hut, he can hit the ball through it and to the green. Is he allowed to do so?

Q12

One of the competitors in a fairly informal competition between company branches decides, at the completion of his round, to play a joke on a couple of his colleagues still playing the course. He hides behind a tree and, after they have teed off and are walking behind a large copse of trees, runs out from his hiding place, removes the pin from the hole and sticks it in the green several yards away. By the time his colleagues come into view again, he has successfully completed his evil deed and is making his way back to the clubhouse.

The players hit their balls to the flag and then discover the joke. Can they replay the balls into the green from their original positions?

Q13

One of the players (Player X) in a four ball match marks his ball about 3 inches behind the ball on the green, saying this will ensure that there is no chance he will accidentally move the ball and incur a penalty under the rules. One of the other players says that although there is not the slightest suggestion that Player X is gaining any advantage, he is wrong in marking the ball in this manner. Is he correct? And, if so, why?

Q14

A ball comes to rest in shallow water in an area clearly within a water hazard, but the player claims that, because the stakes are improperly positioned, his ball is in casual water and he is therefore not subject to the rules governing water hazards. He therefore claims that he is entitled to a free drop away from the water. Is he correct?

Q15

A player usually has a piece of lead tape stuck to the back of his driver to add weight to the club and improve his performance with it. His drives on the first two holes are wayward and, after the second errant shot, he discovers that the tape has been dislodged from the club and is lying in the bottom of the bag.

He re-sticks the tape onto the back of the driver and proceeds to enjoy much better results with it for the rest of the round. But has he run foul of the rules?

Answer:

Although he was taking part in a competition and some could argue that the stroke constituted a practice shot, you will no doubt be delighted to know that Player A's kindly action will not be punished. Because he was acting out of courtesy, the rules say his action was perfectly okay and no penalty has to be paid.

Answer:

Irrespective of whether the practical joker's action has ruined their chances of a better score on this particular hole, the players do not have the option of returning the flag to its correct position in the hole and re-playing their approach shots. They must accept the advantage or disadvantage of the joker's action.

Answer:

Yes he can. Although the hut is officially classed under the rules as an immovable obstruction, its doors and windows are movable and can therefore be opened. Exactly the same ruling would have applied if the ball had come to rest with the clubhouse in a direct line between the ball and the hole.

The unfortunate players will have to accept the joke in good humor and play on.

Answer:

A13

The other player is perfectly correct. By marking his ball 3 inches behind its actual spot, Player X is deemed not to have marked it with enough accuracy. Unfortunately for Player X, he incurs a one-shot penalty every time he marks the ball in this particular way. Incidentally, Player X's fears of being penalized by moving the ball are unfounded. There is no penalty for a ball being accidentally moved while it is marked or lifted in accordance with the rules.

Answer:

A14

No, he is not entitled to a free drop under the terms of relief of casual water. Although the committee has made a mistake in not ensuring that the water hazard is clearly defined by the placement of stakes, the rules do not entitle players to take advantage of the situation. Because it was abundantly clear that the ball was lying within the natural boundaries of the hazard, the player's claim is not valid.

Answer:

A15

Because he started the round with the tape removed from the driver, he has broken the rules, which say that the playing characteristics of a club must not be altered during the course of a round. He is therefore liable for disqualification. If the tape had become detached during the round and in the normal course of play, he would have been allowed to re-stick the tape in exactly the same location.

One common misunderstanding about this rule concerns the use of tape applied to the head of a club during a round to reduce glare from the sun. This is permissible with the rules because the tape is deemed not to change the playing characteristics of a club.

You cannot change the characteristics of your club once you have started to play a round.

As it was clear that the ball was within the natural boundaries of the water hazard, the player cannot have a free drop.

Index

Page numbers in *italics* refer to captions.

Index

CREDITS

Quarto and the authors would like to thank and acknowledge *Today's Golfer* magazine and EMAP Active, Peterborough, for supplying the following photographs reproduced in this book: p2, p7, p16, p44–5, p76–7, p79, p81, and p90–1.
All other photographs and illustrations are the copyright of Quarto Publishing plc.
Quarto and the authors would also like to thank Stoke Park Club, Stoke Poges, Buckinghamshire for allowing us to use the club grounds for photography purposes.
While every effort has been made to credit contributors, Quarto would like to apologize if there have been any omissions or errors.